Acoustic Piano Songs For Dummies

Performance Notes by Bob Gulla and Frank Martyn

ISBN: 978-1-4234-4041-3

7777 W. Bluemound Rd. P.O. Box 13819 Milwaukee, WI 53213

Visit Hal Leonard Online at
www.halleonard.com

Table of Contents

Introduction

Acoustic Piano Songs For Dummies is an amazing collection of songs with melodies a true connoisseur of popular music couldn't possibly resist. Each and every tune qualifies as the kind of chill-inducing song that makes you feel that "certain something" as you listen. Now, we're not exactly sure what to call that "certain something," but we know it when we feel it, and we bet you'll have a similar feeling when you start playing this great music on piano.

In your hands, throughout these pages, are some of pop music's most extraordinary moments, songs created by artists that will live on in our hearts. The Beatles, Tom Petty, Billy Joel, Elton John, Chicago, the Byrds, and other legendary artists all contribute some of their defining musical milestones. Songs like "Yesterday" and "American Pie" rank among the pop-rock canon's best, and wear that most esteemed mantle: classic. Taken together, this collection serves as a gorgeous sonic tapestry of the pop era. And like all classics, each song here places you in a very specific context, a place in time as vivid as your first kiss and just as memorable. (Maybe even *more* memorable if that kiss wasn't so hot.)

About This Book

For every song here, we include a little background or history. Sometimes we discuss the artist, the song, or some other interesting element of the song. This information is followed by a variety of tidbits that struck us as we made our way through the teaching of these songs, including some of the following:

- A run-down of the parts you need to know.
- A breakdown of some of the chord progressions important to playing the song effectively.
- Some of the critical information you need to navigate the sheet music.
- Some tips and shortcuts you can use to expedite the learning process.

In many cases, you may already know how to do a lot of this. If so, feel free to skip over those familiar bits.

How to Use This Book

The music in this book is in standard piano notation — a staff for the melody and lyrics above the traditional piano grand staff. And you'll find the basic chords and their matching *guitar frames.* The frames are diagrams of the guitar strings that show you what frets to play. Even though this book features songs that sound great on piano, you or a friend may also want to learn the accompanying guitar part. We also assume you know a little something about reading music, and that you know a little bit about playing piano (and possibly guitar) — like how to hold your fingers, basic chords, and how to look cool while doing it. If you need a refresher course on piano, please check out *Piano For Dummies* by Blake Neely (Wiley).

We recommend that you first play through the song, and then practice all the main sections and chords. From there, you can add the tricks and treats of each one — and there are many. Approach each song one section at a time and then assemble it together in a sequence. This technique helps to provide you with a greater understanding of how the song is structured, and enables you to play it through more quickly.

In order to follow the music and our performance notes, you need a basic understanding of scales and chords. But if you're not a wiz, don't worry. Just spend a little time with the nifty tome *Music Theory For Dummies* by Michael Pilhofer and Holly Day (Wiley), and with a little practice, you'll be on your way to entertaining family and friends.

Glossary

As you might expect, we use quite a few musical terms in this book. Some of these may be unfamiliar to you, so here are a few right off the bat that can help your understanding of basic playing principles:

- **Arpeggio:** Playing the notes of a chord one at a time rather than all together.
- **Bridge:** Part of the song that is different from the verse and the chorus, providing variety and connecting the other parts of the song to each other.
- **Coda:** The section at the end of a song, which is sometimes labeled with the word "coda."
- **Chorus:** The part of the song that is the same each time through, usually the most familiar section.
- **Hook:** A familiar, accessible, or singalong melody, lick, or other section of the song.
- **Verse:** The part of the song that tells the story; each verse has different lyrics, and each song generally has between two and four of these.

Icons Used in This Book

In the margins of this book are lots of little icons that will help make your life easier:

A reason to stop and review advice that can prevent personal injury to your fingers, your brain, or your ego.

These are optional parts, or alternate approaches that those who'd like to find their way through the song with a distinctive flair can take. Often these are slightly more challenging routes, but encouraged nonetheless, because there's nothing like a good challenge!

This is where you will find notes about specific musical concepts that are relevant but confusing to non-musical types — stuff that you wouldn't bring up, say, at a frat party or at your kid's soccer game.

You get lots of these tips, because the more playing suggestions we can offer, the better you'll play. And isn't that what it's all about?

Amanda

Words and Music by Tom Scholz

G
C/G
And I, I'm get-tin' too close a-
G
Em
Bm
gain. I don't wan-na see it end. If I
C
G/B
Am
G
tell you to-night, will you turn out the light and walk a-way know-in' I love
D
C/D
G/D
D
you? I'm gon-na

Em
Am7
D
take you by sur-prise and make you re - al - ize, A - man - da. I'm gon-na
Em
Am7
D
tell you right a - way; I can't wait an - oth - er day, A - man - da. I'm gon-na
Em
Am7
D
say it like a man and make you un - der - stand, A - man - da. I
Csus2
3fr
love you.
15ma
G
C/G
And I feel like to - day's the

G
Em
Bm
day. I'm look - in' for the words to say. Do you
C
G/B
Am
G
wan - na be free? Are you read - y for me to feel this way? I don't wan - na lose
D
D7sus
G
C/G
ya. So, it may be too soon, I
G
Em
Bm
know. The feel - in' takes so long to grow. If I

C
G/B
Am
G
tell you to - day, will you turn me a - way and let me go?
I don't wan - na lose
D
C/D
G/D
D
Bm
you.
Em
Am7
D
Em
Am7
D
I'm gon - na

Em
Am7
D
take you by sur-prise and make you re - al - ize, A - man - da. I'm gon-na
Em
Am7
D
tell you right a - way; I can't wait an - oth - er day, A - man - da. I'm gon-na
Em
Am7
D
say it like a man and make you un - der - stand, A - man - da. Oh, girl.
E
Bm7

E
Bm7
E
Bm7
You and I, I know that we can't wait. And I swear,
E
Bm7
I swear it's not a lie, girl. To - mor-row may be too late.
C
D
G
D/F♯
Em
Em/D
You, you and I, girl, we can share a life to-geth - er. It's now or nev -

C
C/B
Am
Am/G
D
C/D
- er, and to - mor - row may be too late.
Oh.
G/D
D
G
C/G
And feel - in' the way I
G
Em
Bm
do, I don't wan - na wait my whole life through to
Am
Am/G
D
say I'm in love with you.

American Pie

Words and Music by Don McLean

Em
C
D
may - be they'd be hap - py for a while.
Em
Am
Em
Am
But Feb-ru-ar-y made me shiv-er with ev-'ry pa-per I'd de-liv-er.
C
G/B
Am
C
D
Bad news on the door-step, I could-n't take one more step. I
G
D/F#
Em
Am7
D
can't re-mem-ber if I cried when I read a-bout his wid-owed bride.

G
D/F#
Em
C
D7
G
C/G
Some-thing touched me deep in-side the day the mu-sic died.
Moderately
G
G
C
G
D
So bye - bye Miss A-mer-i-can Pie drove my
G
C
G
D
G
C
Chev-y to the lev-ee but the lev-ee was dry. Them good ole boys were drink-in'
To Coda
G
D
Em
A7
whis-key and rye, sing-in' this-'ll be the day that I die.

Em
D7
This - 'll be the day that I die.
G
Am
1. Did you write the book of love and do you
2.-4. (See additional lyrics)
C
Am
Em
have faith in God a - bove?
If the Bi - ble tells
D
G
D/F#
you so.
Now do you be - lieve in

Em
Em/D
Am7
C
rock and roll? Can mu - sic save your mor - tal soul and
Em
A7
D
can you teach me how to dance real slow?
Em
D
Well, I know that you're in love with him 'cause I
Em
D
C
G/B
A
saw you danc - in' in the gym. You both kicked off your shoes.

C
D7
Man, I dig those rhy - thm and blues. I was a
G
D/F♯
Em
Am
lone - ly teen - age bronc - in' buck with a pink car - na - tion and a
C
G
D/F♯
Em
pick - up truck. But I knew I was out of luck the day
C
D7
G
C
G
the mu - sic died.

1 - 3
4
D7
D7
G
C
I start - ed sing - ing
He was sing - in' bye - bye Miss A -
G
D
G
C
G
D
mer - i - can Pie drove my Chev - y to the lev - ee but the lev - ee was dry. Them
G
C
G
D
good ole boys were drink - in' whis - key and rye, sing - in'
Em
A7
this - 'll be the day that I die.

Em
D7
This-'ll be the day that I die.
rit.
Freely
G
D/F♯
Em7
Am
C
I met a girl who sang the blues and I asked her for some hap-py news, but
Em
D
she just smiled and turned a - way.
G
D/F♯
Em
G/B
Am
G/B
C
I went down to the sa-cred store where I heard the mu - sic years be-fore, but the

Em C D
man there said the mu - sic would-n't play. And
Em Am Em Am
in the streets the chil - dren screamed, the lov - ers cried and the po - ets dreamed. But
C G/B Am C D G D/F♯ Em G/B
not a word was spo - ken, the church bells all were bro - ken. And the three men I ad - mire most, the
C D7 G D/F♯ Em
Fa - ther, Son and the Ho - ly Ghost, they caught the last train for the coast the

Additional Lyrics

2. Now for ten years we've been on our own,
And moss grows fat on a rollin' stone
But that's not how it used to be
When the jester sang for the king and queen
In a coat he borrowed from James Dean
And a voice that came from you and me
Oh and while the king was looking down,
The jester stole his thorny crown
The courtroom was adjourned,
No verdict was returned
And while Lenin read a book on Marx
The quartet practiced in the park
And we sang dirges in the dark
The day the music died
We were singin'...bye-bye...etc.

3. Helter-skelter in the summer swelter
The birds flew off with a fallout shelter
Eight miles high and fallin' fast,
It landed foul on the grass
The players tried for a forward pass,
With the jester on the sidelines in a cast
Now the half-time air was sweet perfume
While the sergeants played a marching tune
We all got up to dance
But we never got the chance
'Cause the players tried to take the field,
The marching band refused to yield
Do you recall what was revealed
The day the music died
We started singin'... bye-bye...etc.

4. And there we were all in one place,
A generation lost in space
With no time left to start again
So come on, Jack be nimble, Jack be quick,
Jack Flash sat on a candlestick
'Cause fire is the devil's only friend
And as I watched him on the stage
My hands were clenched in fits of rage
No angel born in hell
Could break that Satan's spell
And as the flames climbed high into the night
To light the sacrificial rite
I saw Satan laughing with delight
The day the music died
He was singin'...bye-bye...etc.

At Seventeen

Words and Music by Janis Ian

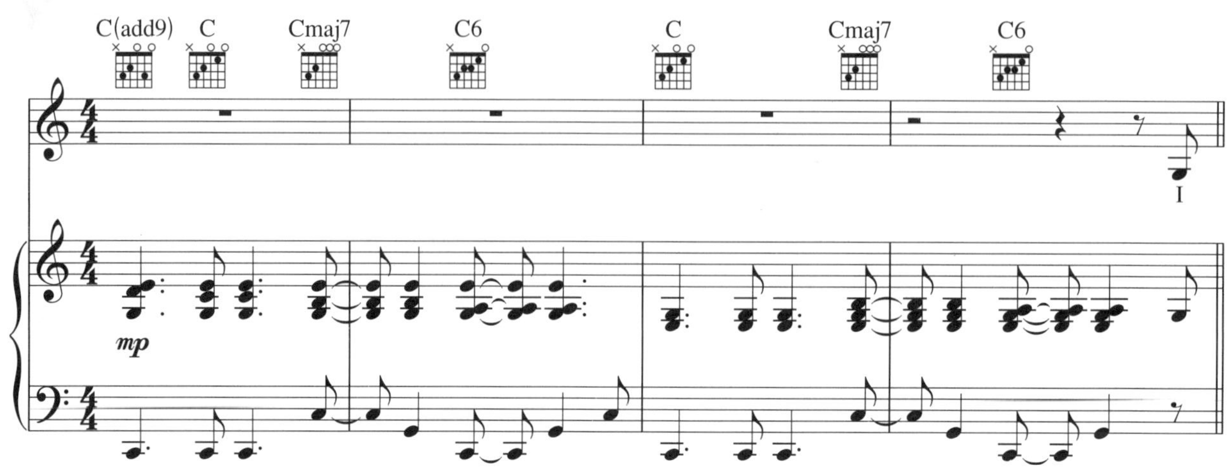

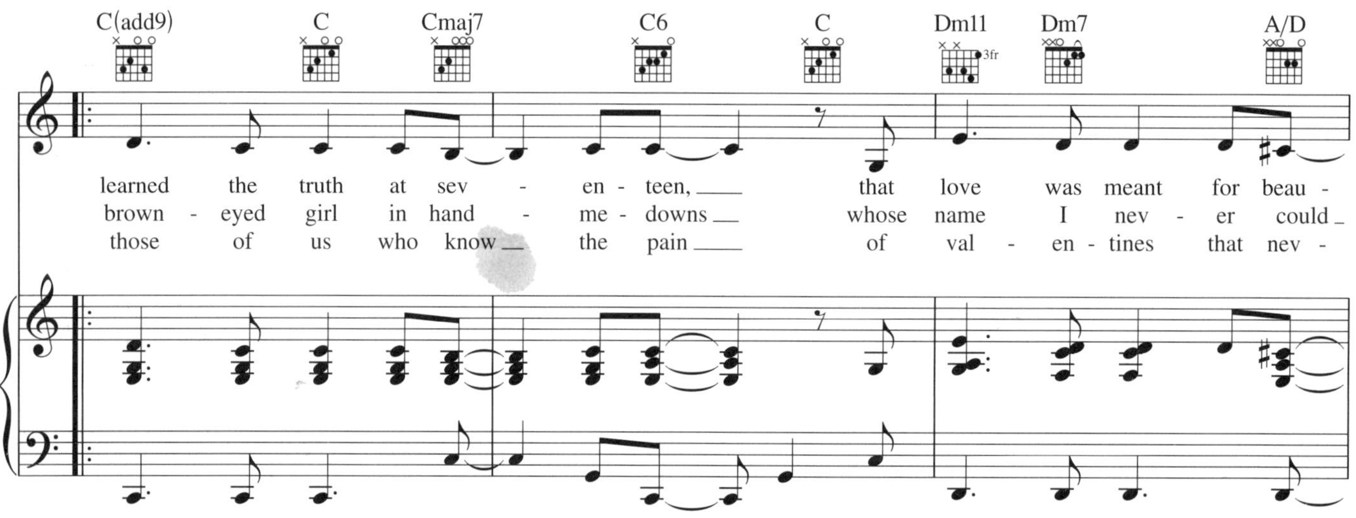

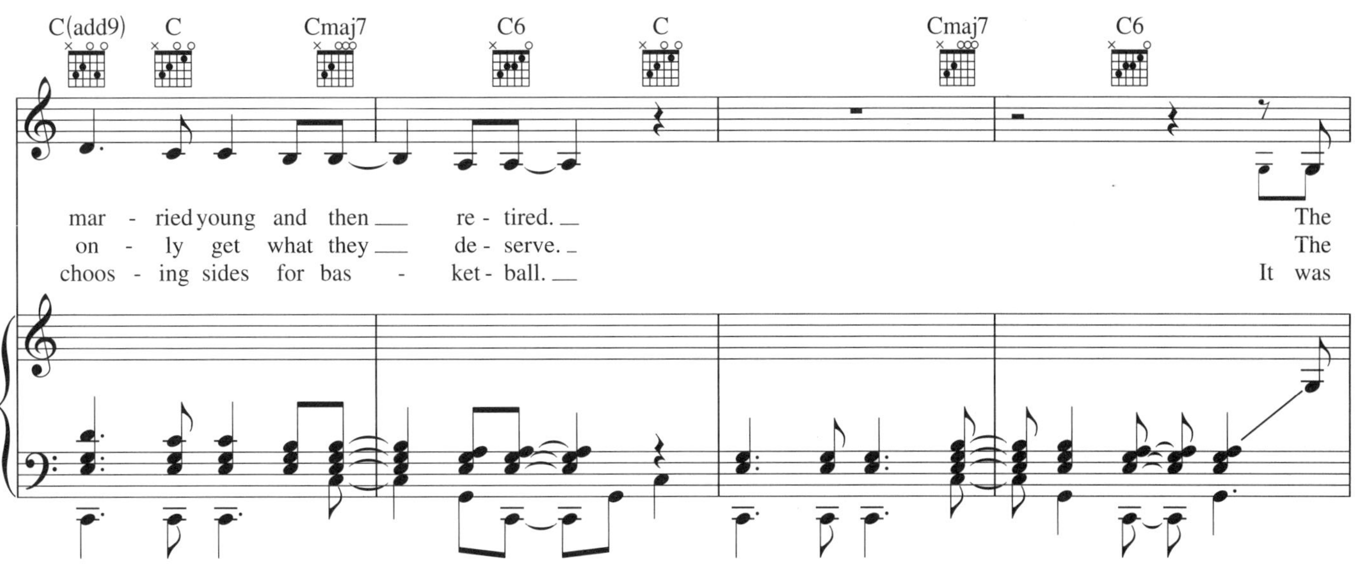
C(add9)
C
Cmaj7
C6
C
Cmaj7
C6
mar - ried young and then re - tired. The
on - ly get what they de - serve. The
choos - ing sides for bas - ket - ball. It was

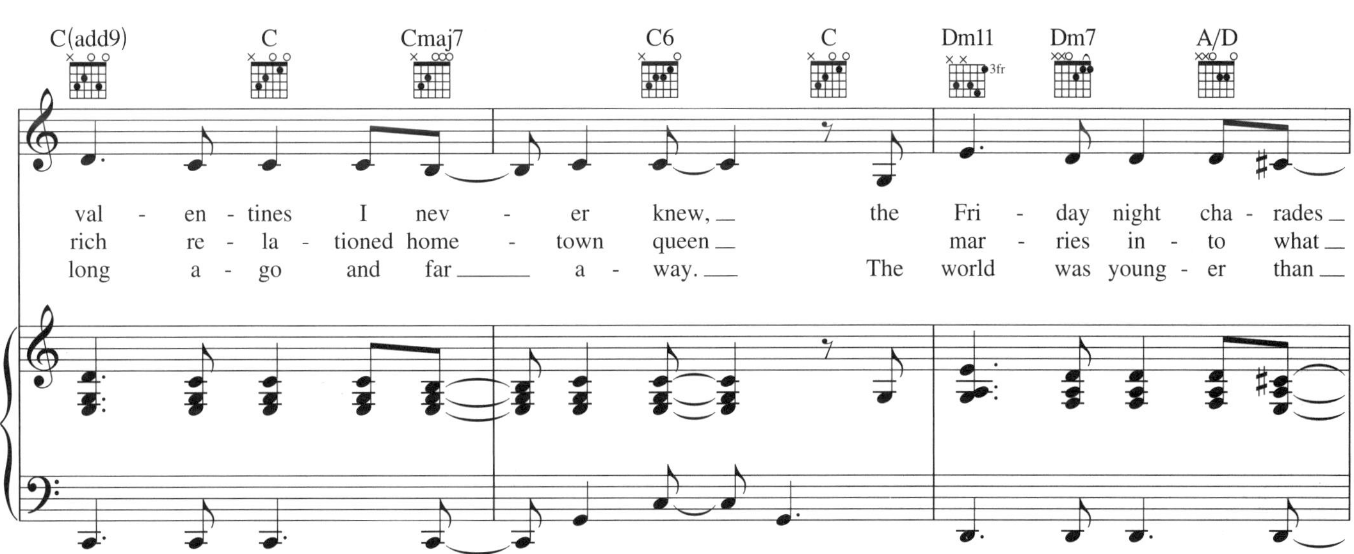
C(add9)
C
Cmaj7
C6
C
Dm11
3fr
Dm7
A/D
val - en - tines I nev - er knew, the Fri - day night cha - rades
rich re - la - tioned home - town queen mar - ries in - to what
long a - go and far a - way. The world was young - er than

Dm7
G7
of youth were spent on one more beau - ti - ful, at
she needs, a guar - an - tee of com - pa - ny and
to - day, and dreams were all they gave for free to

C(add9)
C
Cmaj7
C
C(add9)
C
Cmaj7
C
sev - en - teen, I learned the truth.
ha - ven for the el - der - ly."
ug - ly duck - ling girls like me.
And
Re -
We all

E♭
3fr
Dm7
those of us with rav - aged fac - es,
mem - ber those who win the game,
play the game and when we dare to
lack - ing in the so -
lose the love they sought
cheat our - selves at sol -

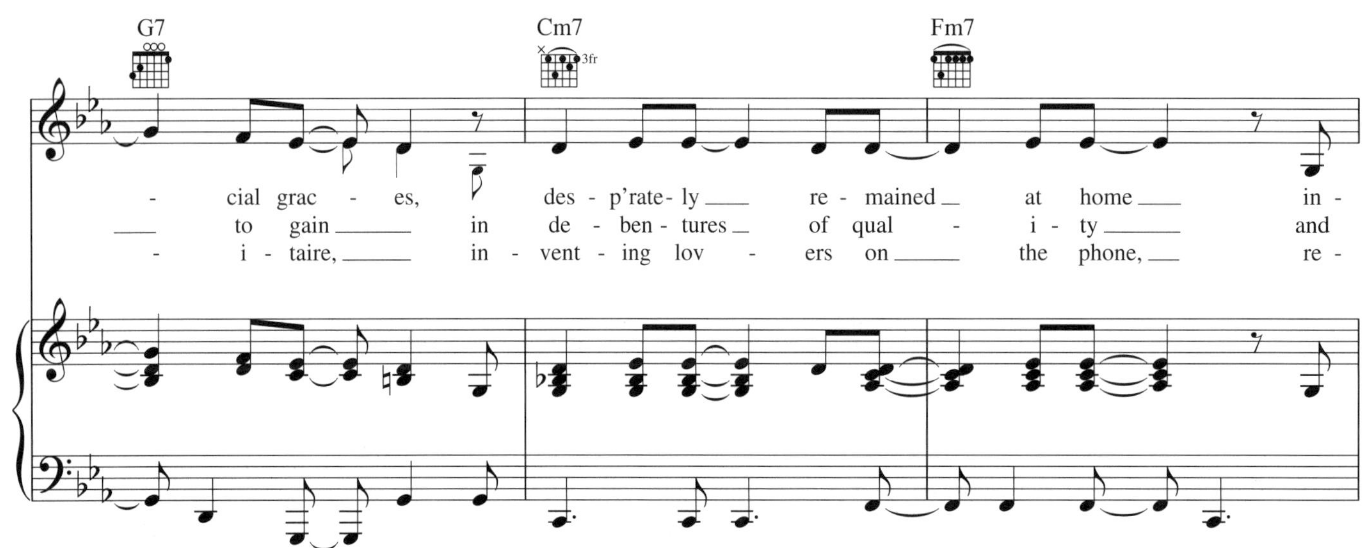
G7
Cm7
3fr
Fm7
- cial grac - es,
to gain in
- i - taire,
des - p'rate - ly re - mained at home in -
de - ben - tures of qual - i - ty and
in - vent - ing lov - ers on the phone, re -

Cm7
Fm7
A♭
3fr
4fr
vent - ing lov - ers on the phone who called to say, "Come dance
du - bi - ous in - teg - ri - ty. Their small town eyes will gape
pent - ing oth - er lives un - known that call and say, "Come dance
G7
Cm7
Fm7
with me," and mur - mured vague ob - scen - i - ties.
at you in dull sur - prise when pay - ment due
with me," and mur - mur vague ob - scen - i - ties
Dm7
G7
1, 2
It is - n't all it seems at sev - en - teen. A
ex - ceeds ac - counts re - ceived at sev - en - teen. To
at ug - ly girls like me at sev - en - teen.
3
C(add9)
C
Cmaj7
C
Cmaj7

Blackbird

Words and Music by John Lennon and Paul McCartney

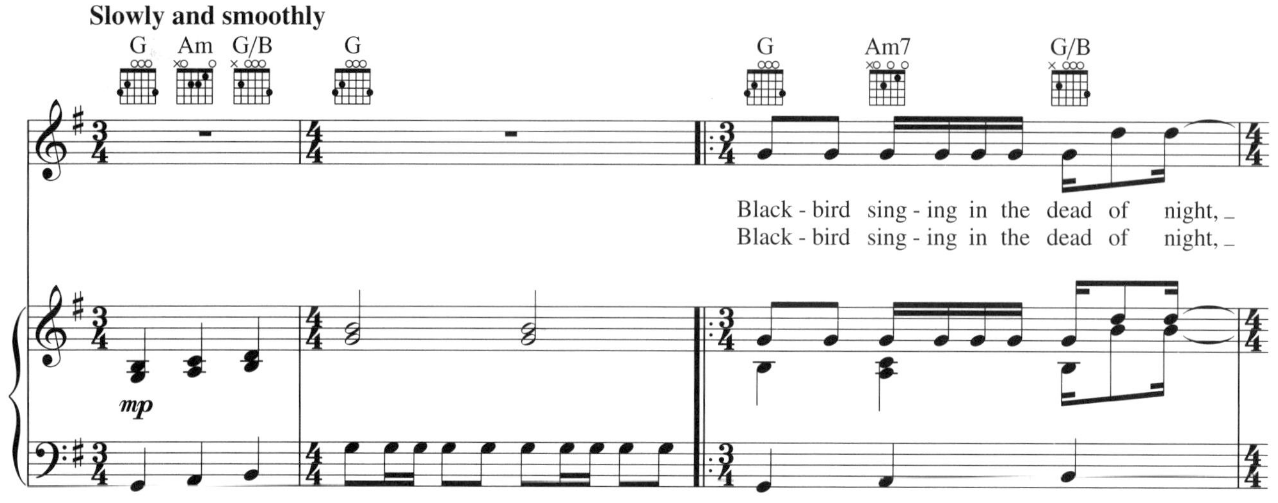

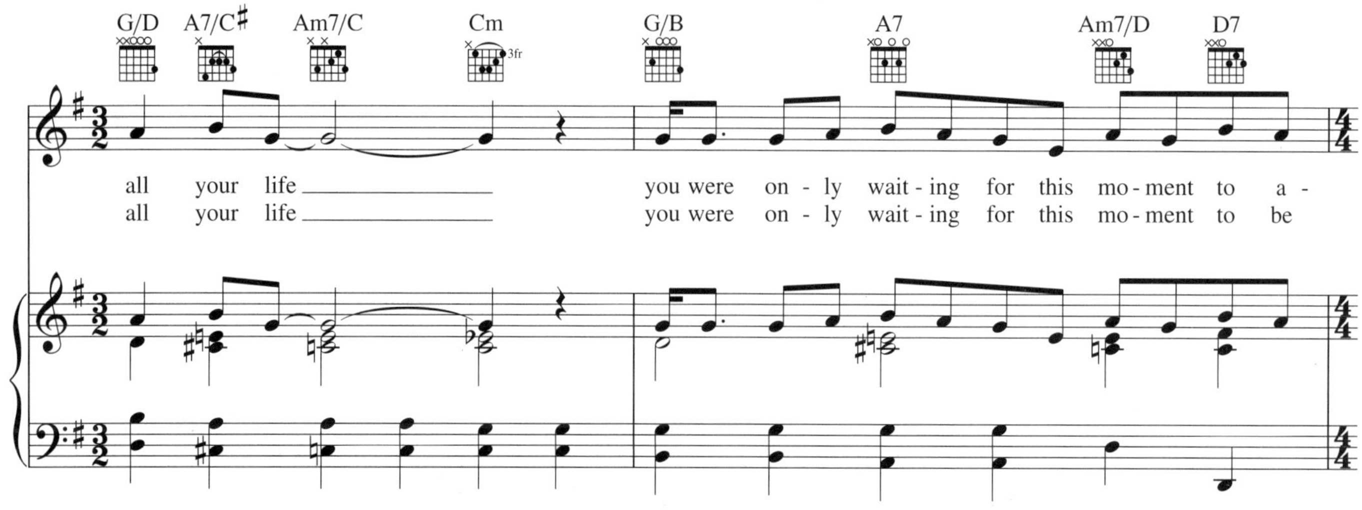

1
G
C
G/B
A7
D7
G
2
G
rise.
free.
F
C/E
Dm
C
B♭
C
F
C/E
Dm
C
Black - bird, fly,
black - bird, fly
B♭
A7
D7
G
Am7
G/B
in - to the light of a dark black night.
G
C
A7/C♯
D7
B7/D♯
Em
Cm/E♭
3fr

Gmaj7/D
A7/C♯
Am7/C
Cm
G/B
A7
D7
G
F
C/E
Dm
C
B♭
C
Black - bird, fly,
black - bird, fly
B♭
A7
D7
G
Am7
G/B
in - to the light of a dark black night.
G
molto rit.
a tempo
G
A7
G/B
C
G/B
A7

Am7/D
G
Am7
G/B
G
Black-bird sing-ing in the dead of night,
C
A7/C♯
D7
B7/D♯
Em
Cm/E♭
3fr
G/D
A7/C♯
Am7/C
Cm
3fr
take these bro-ken wings and learn to fly;
all your life
G/B
A7
Am7/D
D7
G
C
G/B
A7
you were on-ly wait-ing for this mo-ment to a-rise.
You were on-ly wait-ing for this
Am7/D
D7
G
C
G/B
A7
Am7/D
D7
G
mo-ment to a-rise.
You were on-ly wait-ing for this
mo-ment to a-rise.

Candle in the Wind

Words and Music by Elton John and Bernie Taupin

A
and they whis-pered in - to your brain. They set you on the tread -
oh, the press still hound-ed you. All the pa - pers had
E/G#
A
D/A
- mill and they made you change your name.
to say was that Mar - i - lyn was found in the nude.
A
B
B7
And it seems to me you lived your life like a
E
A
E
can - dle in the wind, nev - er know-ing who to cling

B
Bsus
B
to when the rain set in.
And I
A
C♯m
4fr
would have liked to have known you, but I was just a kid.
Your
B
Bsus
B
can - dle burned out long be - fore
your
A
A/G♯
F♯m7
E
leg - end ev - er did.

B
A
A/G♯
F♯m7
E
Esus
E
1
B
B7
2
B
B7/A
E
Good-bye Nor - ma Jean,
A
though I nev - er knew you at all, you had the grace to
E/G♯
A
D/A
hold your - self while those a - round you crawled.

A
E
Good-bye Nor - ma Jean, from the young man in the
A
E/G♯
twen - ty sec - ond row who sees you as some-thing more than sex - ual, more than
A
Asus
A
just our Mar - i - lyn Mon - roe. And it
B
B7
E
E7
seems to me you lived your life like a can - dle in the wind,

A
E
never knowing who to cling to when the rain
B
Bsus
B
A
set in. And I would have liked to have known
C♯m
4fr
you, but I was just a kid. Your candle burned out
B
Bsus
B
A
long before your legend ever did.

A/G♯
F♯7
E
E7/G♯
I
A
C♯m
4fr
would have liked to have known you, whoa, but I was just a kid.
B
Your can - dle burned out long be - fore
Bsus
B
A
A/G♯
F♯m7
E
your leg-end ev - er did.
rit.

Crazy Little Thing Called Love

Words and Music by Freddie Mercury

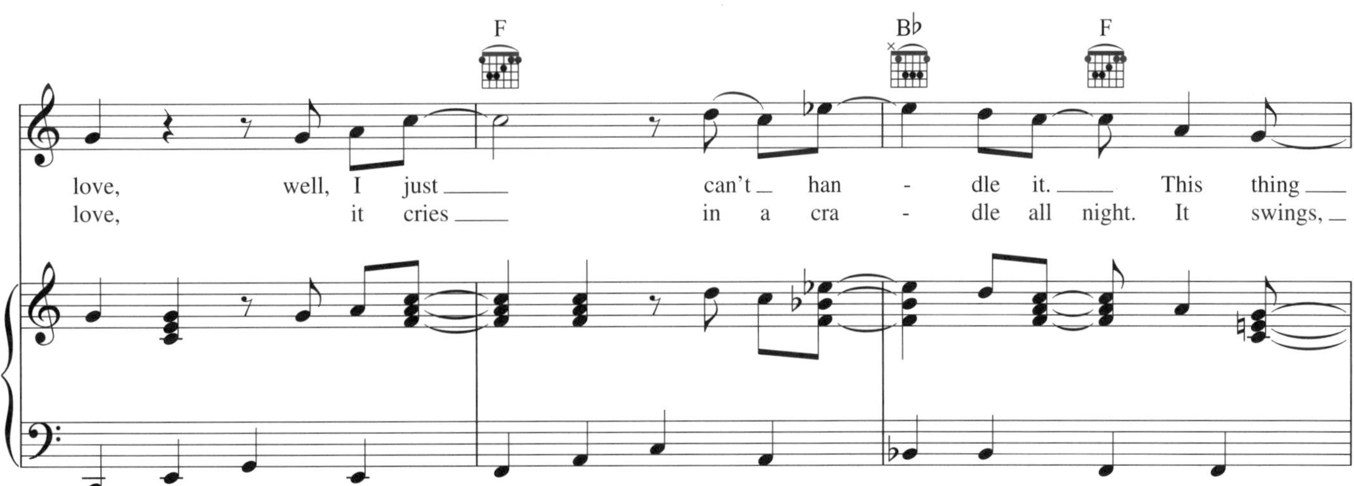

Bb
F
C
Ab
4fr
Bb
round to it. I ain't ready.
jel - ly - fish. I kind - a like it.
Cra - zy lit - tle thing called
C
1
N.C.
2
N.C.
F7
love.
Well, this thing
There goes my ba - by;
Bb
F
she knows how to rock and roll. She drives me
Ab
4fr
D7
G
cra - zy.
She gives me hot and cold fe - ver. She

N.C.
leaves me in a cool, cool sweat.
C
I got - ta be cool, re - lax,
F
a - get hip, a - get
B♭
F
on my tracks. Take a
C
back seat, hitch - hike
F
and take a long ride on a

B♭
F
C
A♭
B♭
4fr
mo - tor bike un - til I'm read - y. Cra - zy lit - tle thing called
C
N.C.
A♭
4fr
love.
C
3
3
A♭
4fr
D7

G
N.C.
I got - ta be cool, relax,
a - get hip, a - get on my tracks. Take a
back seat, hitch - hike to take a lit - tle long ride on my

mo - tor bike un - til I'm read - y. Cra - zy lit - tle thing called
love. This thing called
C
love, I just can't han - dle it. This
F
B♭
F
thing called love, I must get a -
C
F

B♭
F
C
A♭
4fr
round to it. I ain't ready - y. Cra - zy lit - tle thing called
love, cra - zy lit - tle thing called love, cra -
- zy lit - tle thing called love, cra - zy lit - tle thing called
love, hey, cra - zy lit - tle thing called love.
C6/9
3

Change the World

Words and Music by Wayne Kirkpatrick, Gordon Kennedy and Tommy Sims

A/E
E7(no3rd)
shine it on my heart
I'd take you as my queen,
A/E
E
so you could see the truth,
I'd have it no oth - er way.
A
D/A
A7(no3)
2fr
then this love I have in - side
And our love will rule in this
D/A
A
is ev - 'ry - thing it seems.
king - dom we have made.

E
A/E
E7(no3rd)
But for now I find
'Til then I'd be a fool
A/E
G♯7
's on - ly in my dreams
wish - ing for the day
that I can
F♯m7
G♯7
C♯m7
change the world.
D♯m7♭5
G♯7
C♯m
I will would would be the sun - light in your u - ni - verse.

D♯m7♭5
G♯7
C♯m
Cm
Bm9
You would think my love was real - ly some - thing good, ba - by,
To Coda
A
E(add9)/G♯
1
Edim/G
F♯m7
if I could change the world.
E
A/E
Em7
A/E
E
2
Edim/G
F♯m7
change the world,

E
A7sus
E(add9)/G♯
Edim/G
3fr
F♯m7(add4)
ba - by, if I could change
the world.
Guitar solo
A/E
G
F♯m7
G♯7
4fr
D.S. al Coda
Solo ends I could

CODA
Edim/G
F♯m7
A
E(add9)/G♯
change the world, ba - by, if I could
Edim/G
F♯m7
A
E(add9)/G♯
E(add9)/G♯
Edim/G
change the world, ba - by, if I could change
Esus/F♯
G6
E
F♯m7
G
the world.
3fr
F♯m7
E

Don't Let the Sun Go Down on Me

Words and Music by Elton John and Bernie Taupin

G
C/G
G
C/G
G
C/G
I'm grow-ing tired
G7
F/C
C
C7/E
and time stands still be - fore me.
F
B♭/F
F
Fro - zen here, on the lad - der of my
G
C/G
G7
life.

C/G
G7
C
F/C
Too late to save my-self from fall - ing.
C
C7/E
F
B♭/F
I took a chance
F
G
C/G
G
and changed your way of life.
G7
C/G
G
F/C
C
But you mis-read my mean-ing when I met you.

C7/E
F
Closed the door and left me blind-
-ed by the light.
C/G
G
F/G
C
C/B♭
Don't let the sun go down on me.
Am7
D7/F♯
Al-though I search my-self, it's al-ways some-one else I see.

C/G
F/G
G7
I'd just al - low a frag - ment of your life to wan - der free.
C
C/B♭
But
F/A
Dm
C/E
F
C/G
F/G
To Coda
los - ing ev - 'ry - thing is like the sun go - ing down on
C
C/B♭
F/A
C/G
me.

F
G
C/G
G7
I can't find oh the right ro-
C
C7/E
F
man-tic line. But see me once
G7
C/G
G7
and see the way I feel.
C/G
G7
Don't dis-card me just be-cause you think

C
C/E
I mean you harm.
F
C/G
But these cuts I have,
oh, they need
love
to help them
G
G7
D.S. al Coda
heal.
CODA
C
C/B♭
me.
F/A
A♭
4fr
B♭
C

Give a Little Bit

Words and Music by Rick Davies and Roger Hodgson

A7
G
A7
G
Bm
to you.
for you.
There's so much that we need
Now's the time that we need
Esus
E
To Coda
G
Bm/A
A7
to share, so send a smile and show you care.
to share, so
D/A
A7
D
A7
I'll give a lit - tle bit,
D
G
A7
G
I'll give a lit - tle bit of my life for you.

A7
G
D
A7
So, give a lit - tle bit,
D
G
A7
G
oh, give a lit - tle bit of your time to me.
A7
G
Bm
Esus
E
See the man with the lone - ly eyes? Oh,
G
Bm/A
A7
D/A
A7
take his hand; you'll be sur - prised.

F♯m7
Bm
F♯m7
Sax solo ad lib.
Bm
F♯m7
G
C
G
A
D/A
A
D/A
(Ah.
A
D/A
A
D/A
A
D/A
Ah.
Ah.)

A
A7
D.S. al Coda
Solo ends
CODA
G
find your - self; we're on
C
G
A
D/A
our way back home.
Oh, go - in' home.
Don't you need, don't you need to feel at home?
D
G/D
A/D
Oh, yeah, we got - ta sing.

Dust in the Wind

Words and Music by Kerry Livgren

Moderate Folk style

C
G/B
Am
close my eyes
Same old song.
don't hang on.
G
Dm7
Am
G/B
on - ly for a mo - ment, and the mo - ment's gone.
Just a drop of wa - ter in an end - less sea.
Noth - ing lasts for - ev - er but the earth and sky. It
C
G/B
Am
All my dreams
All we do
slips a - way.
G
Dm7
Am
To Coda
pass be - fore my eyes, a cu - ri - os - i - ty.
crum - bles to the ground, though we re - fuse to see.
All your mon - ey won't an - oth - er min - ute buy.

D/F#
G
Am
Am/G
Dust in the wind.
Dust in the wind.
1
D/F#
G
Am
G/B
All they are is dust in the wind.
2
D/F#
G
Am
All we are is dust in the wind.
G/A
3fr
F/A
Oh.

Am
G/A
3fr
F/A

1
2

C

1
Am

2
D.S. al Coda
Am
G/B
Now,
CODA
D/F♯
G
Am
Am/G
Dust in the wind.
All we are is dust in the wind.
(All we are is dust in the wind.)
Dust in the wind.
(Ev - 'ry - thing is dust in the

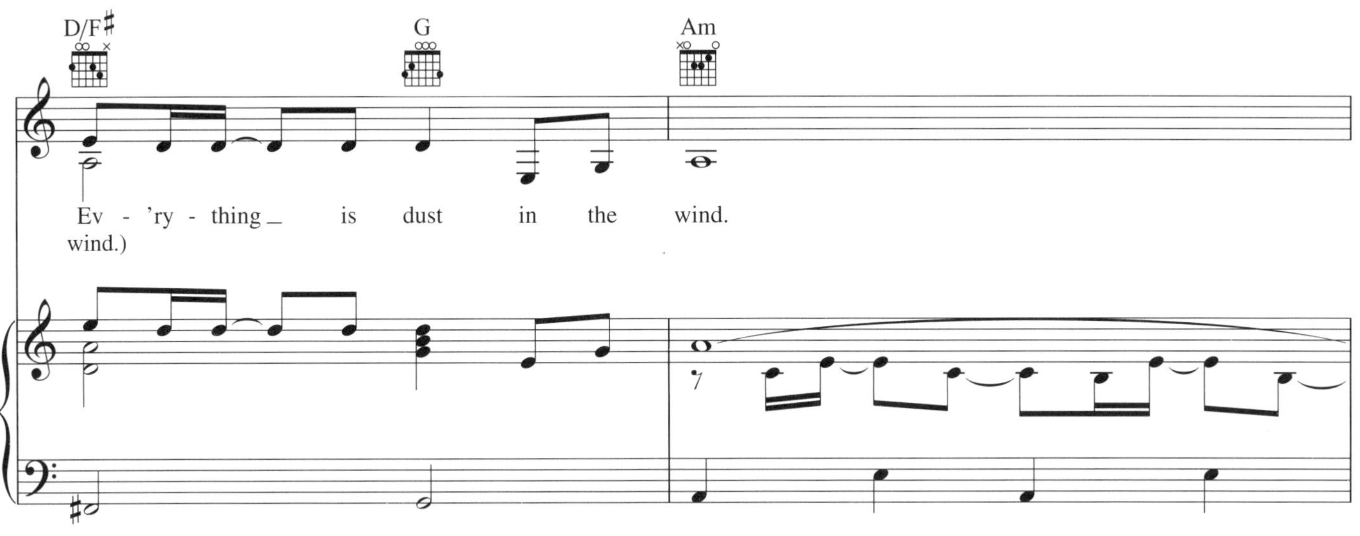

Repeat and Fade

Free Fallin'

Words and Music by Tom Petty and Jeff Lynne

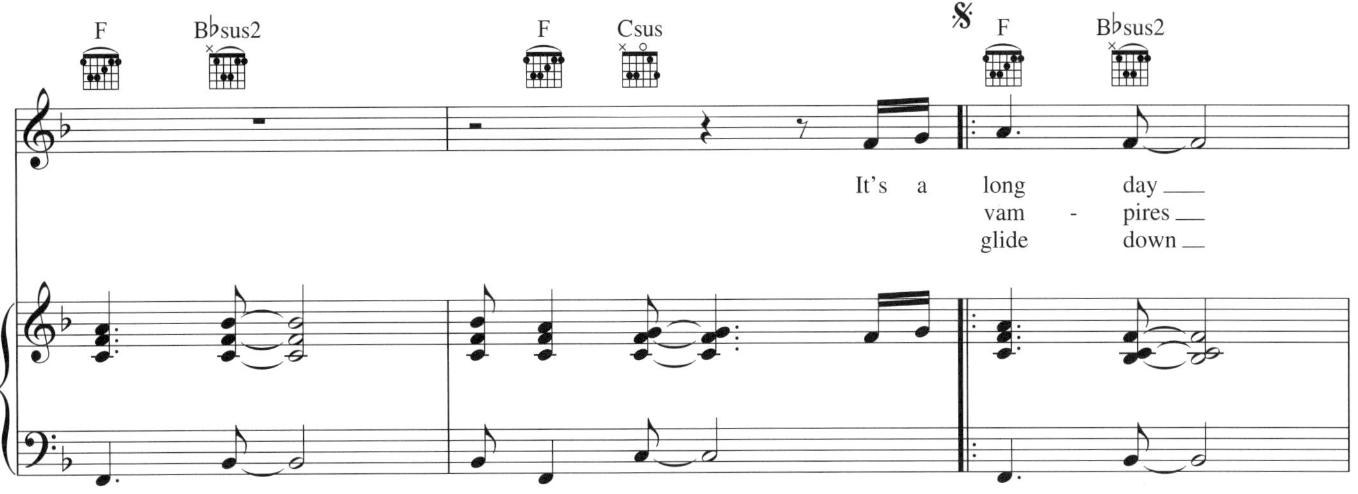
F
B♭sus2
F
Csus
F
B♭sus2
It's a long day
vam - pires
glide down

F
Csus
F
B♭sus2
F
Csus
liv - in' in Re - se - da. There's a free - way run - nin' through the yard. And I'm a
walk - in' through the val - ley move west down Ven - tur - a Boul - e - vard. And all the
o - ver Mul - hol - land. I wan - na write her name in the sky. I wan - na

F
B♭sus2
F
Csus
F
B♭sus2
bad boy 'cause I don't e - ven miss her. I'm a bad boy for
bad boys are stand - ing in the shad - ows. And the good girls are
free fall out in - to noth - in'. Gon - na leave this

F
Csus
Bbsus2
break - in' her heart.
home with bro - ken hearts.
world for a while.
And I'm free,
free
fall - in'.
Yeah, I'm free,
To Coda
1
free fall - in'.
All the
2
Instrumental solo

F
B♭sus2
1
F
Csus
2
F
Csus
D.S. al Coda
Solo ends
Wan-na
CODA
F
Csus
And I'm
F
B♭sus2
free,
F
Csus
free
F
B♭sus2
fall - in'.
F
Csus
Yeah, I'm
F
B♭sus2
free,
F
Csus
free
F
B♭sus2
fall - in'.
Repeat and Fade
F
Csus
And I'm
Optional Ending
F
Csus

Have You Ever Seen the Rain?

Words and Music by John Fogerty

When it's o - ver, so they say, it - 'll rain a sun -
- ny day. I know; shin - in' down like wa - ter.
G
C
F
G
I want to know, have you
C
Am
F
ev - er seen the rain? I want to

G
C
Am
know,
have you
ev - er
seen
the
rain
F
Gsus
3fr
To Coda
C
com - in'
down
on a
sun - ny
day?
Yes - ter - day,
and
days
be - fore,
sun
is
cold
and
rain
is
hard.
I
know;
G
been
that
way
for
all

C
my time.
'Til for - ev - er, on
it goes
through the cir - cle, fast
and slow.
I know;
G
C
and it can't stop,
I won - der.
D.S. al Coda
CODA
C
G
C

Honesty

Words and Music by Billy Joel

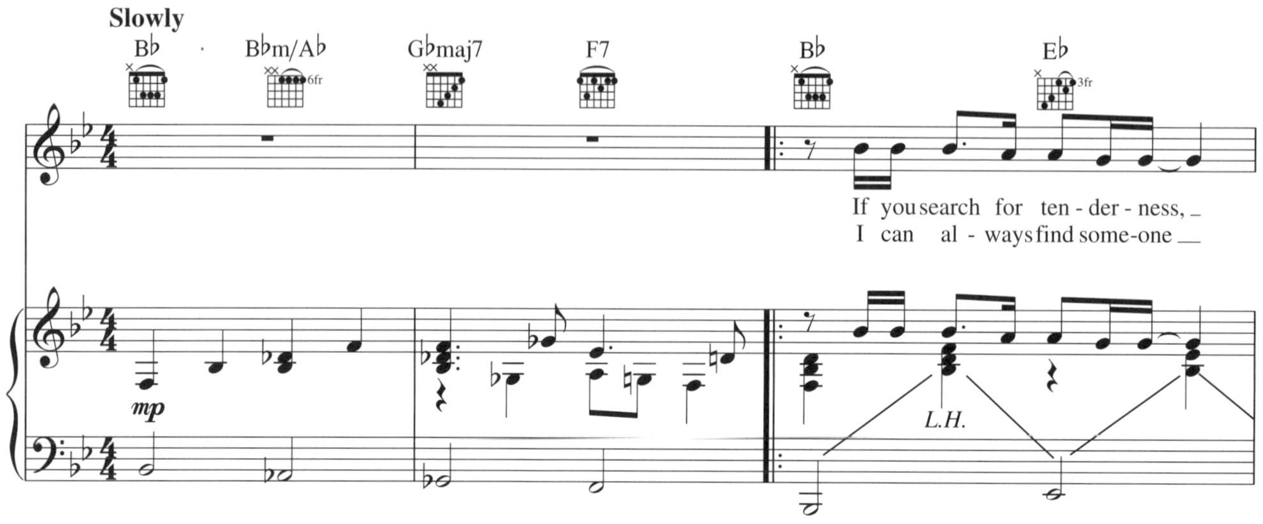

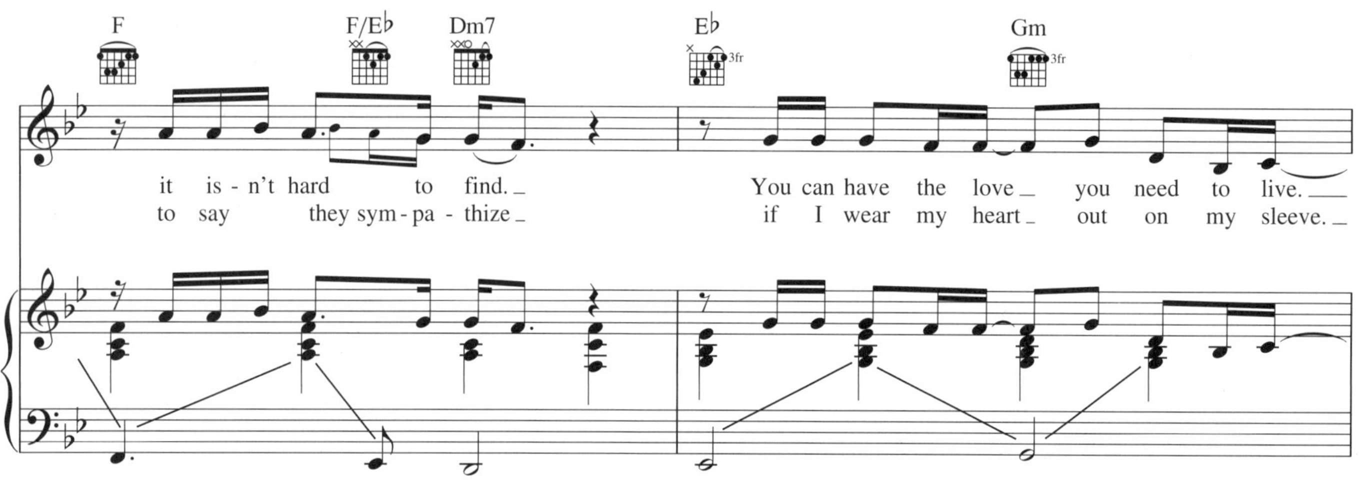

F/C
A/C♯
Dm
E♭
A7
just as well be blind; it al-ways seems to be so hard to give.
tell me pret - ty lies. All I want is some - one to be - lieve.
Dsus
D
E♭maj7
F7
D/F♯
Gm7
F
Hon - es-ty is such a lone - ly word.
E♭
F
B♭
D
E♭maj7
F7
Ev-'ry-one is so un-true. Hon - es-ty is

To Coda
D/F♯
Gm7
F
E♭
3fr
F
Cm/F
Cm/B♭
3fr
8fr
hard - ly ev - er heard,
but most - ly what I need from you.

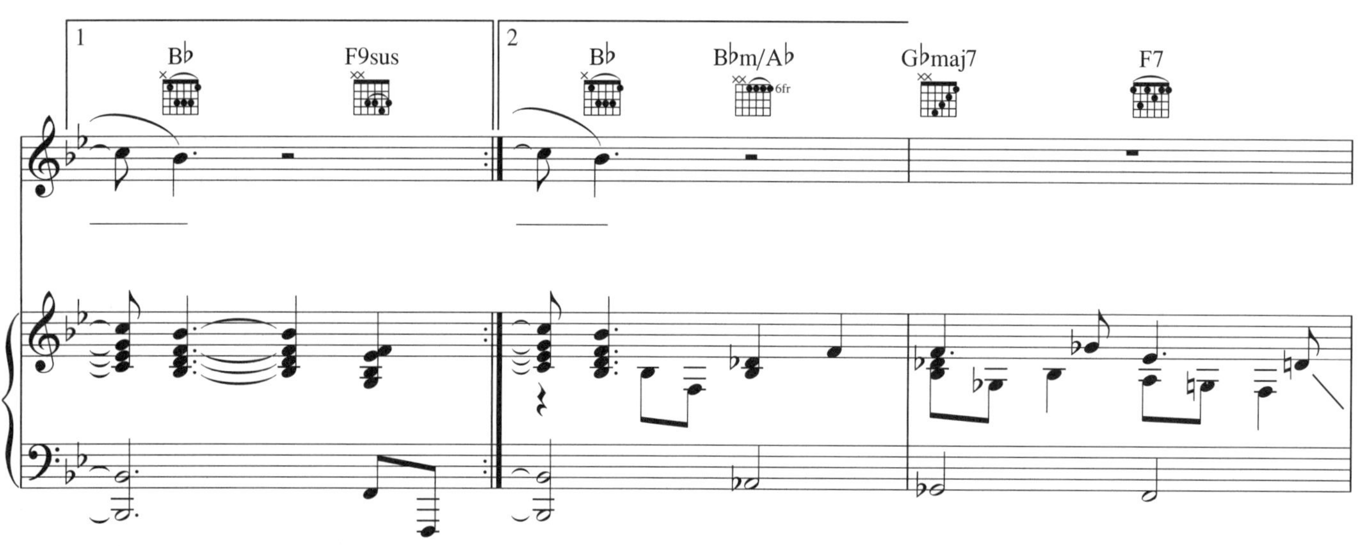
1
B♭
F9sus
2
B♭
B♭m/A♭
6fr
G♭maj7
F7

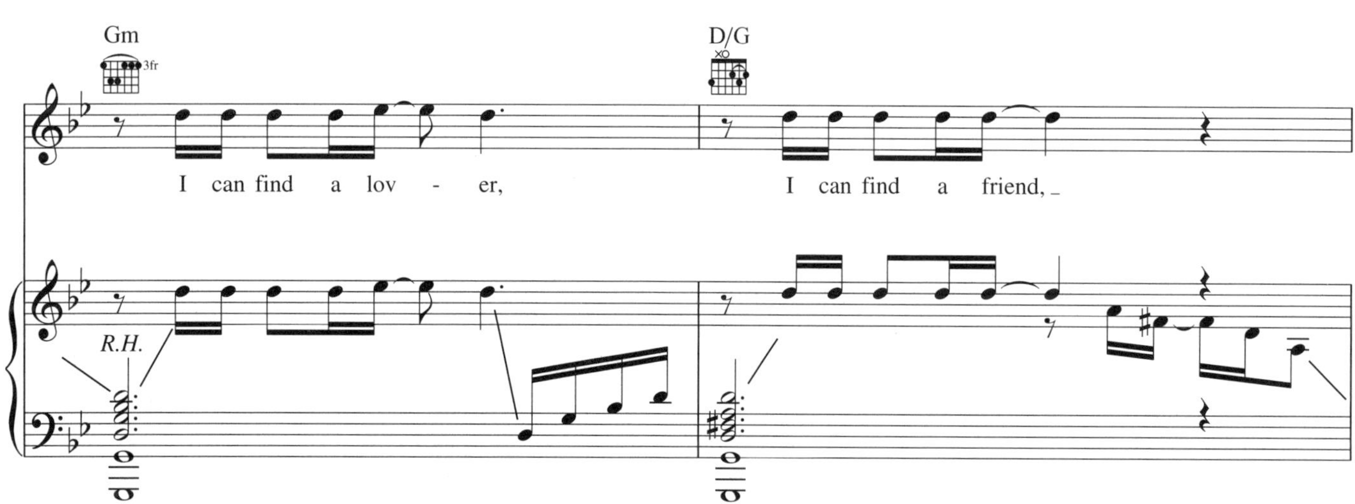
Gm
3fr
D/G
I can find a lov - er,
I can find a friend,
R.H.

Fm6
C7/E
I can have se - cur - i - ty un - til the bit - ter end.
E♭
F
F7
E♭/B♭
B♭
An - y - one can com - fort me with prom - is - es a - gain I know,
C7sus
C7
F
D/F♯
D
E♭
F9sus
I know.
B♭
E♭
F
F/E♭
Dm
When I'm deep in - side of me don't be too con - cerned.

Eb
Gm
Am
Cm7
F
F7
I won't ask for noth - in' while I'm gone.
Bb
Csus
C
F/C
A/C#
Dm
When I want sin - cer - i - ty, tell me, where else can I turn? 'Cause
Eb
A7
D7sus
D7
D.S. al Coda
you're the one that I de - pend up - on.
CODA
Bb
Bbm/Ab
Gbmaj7
F7
Ebm(maj7)
F6
F7
Bb

I'll Follow the Sun

Words and Music by John Lennon and Paul McCartney

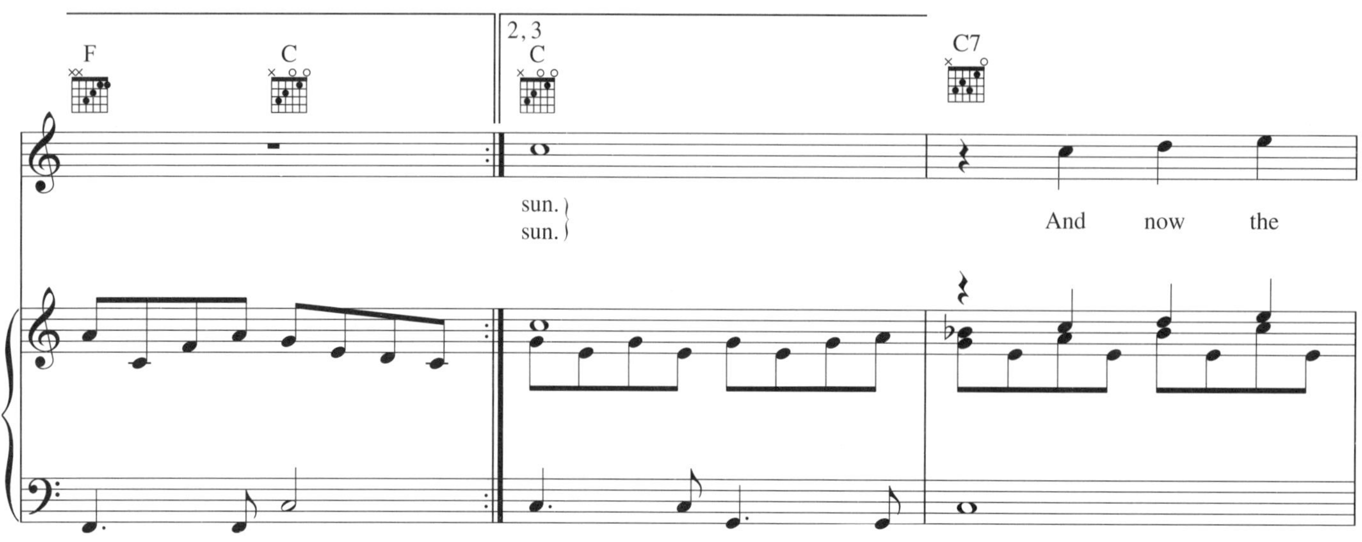
F
C
2, 3
C
C7
sun.
sun.
And now the

Dm
Fm6
C
time has come, and so, my love, I must go.

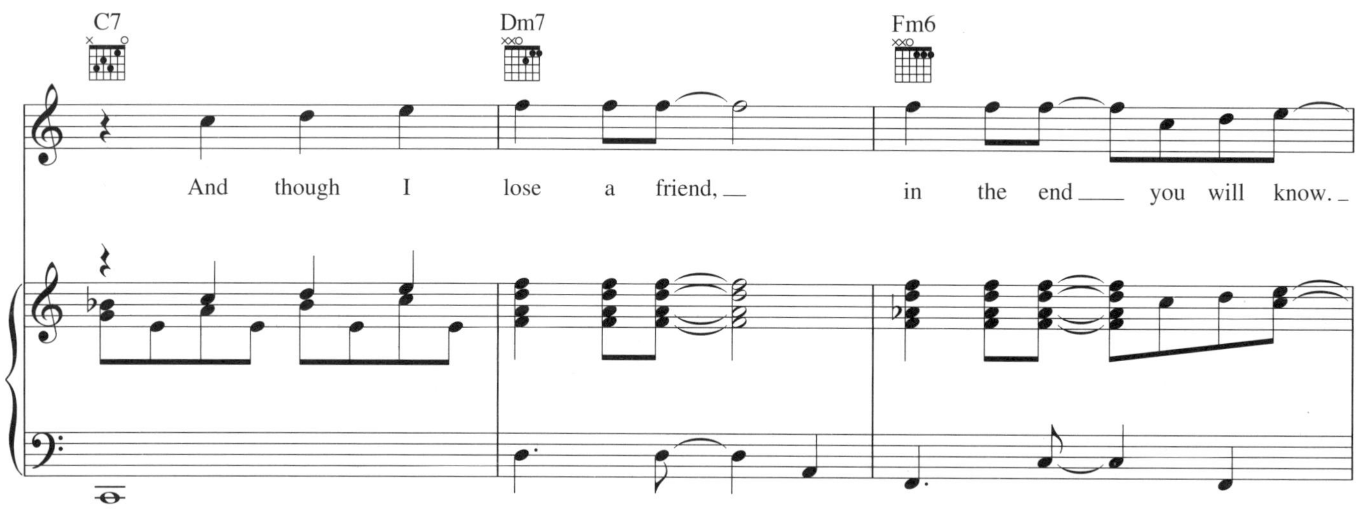
C7
Dm7
Fm6
And though I lose a friend, in the end you will know.

C
Dm7
G
Oh,
one
day
F7
C
D7
you'll
find
that
I
have
gone,
but, to -
C
Em/B
D7
G7
To Coda
C
Dm7/G
mor - row may rain,
so
I'll
fol - low
the
sun.
F
C
D.S. al Coda
(take 2nd ending)
CODA
C
Dm7/G
F
C
sun.

If You Leave Me Now

Words and Music by Peter Cetera

2
C
Am7
D7
3
Ooh, girl, I just want you to stay.
C
G
C
F9sus
A love
We've come
B♭m/F
F
like ours is love that's hard to find.
too far to leave it all be - hind.
Am7
F
G
1, 3
C
How could we let it slip a - way?
How could we end it all this way?

E
2, 4
C
Em7
When to - mor - row comes then we'll both
Am7
Dm
Em
Fm
To Coda
re - gret the things we said to - day.
Cmaj7
Am7
Em7
Am7
D

G
C
Am7
D7
G
C
G
C
D.S. al Coda
(with repeats)
CODA
If you
Cmaj7
Am7
Em7
leave me now, you'll take a - way the big - gest part of me.
Am7
D7
G
Ooh. no, ba - by, please don't go.

C
Am7
D
G
C
G
C
G
C
G
C
Am7
D7
Ooh, girl, just
Ooh, ma - ma, just
G
C
Am7
D7
got to have you by my side.
got to have your lov - in'.
G
C
G
C
G
C
G
C
Repeat and Fade
Ooh,

Jack and Diane

Words and Music by John Mellencamp

D
E
A
E
in the heart - land.
Jack, he's gon - na be
a foot - ball star.
D
E
A
E
Di - ane's deb - u - tante back seat of Jack - y's car.
D
E
A
E/A
D/A
E/A

A
E/A
D/A
A
A
E
Suck - in' on a chil - li dog out -
Jack, he sit back, col - lects his
mp
D
E
A
E
side the Tas - tee Freez;
thoughts for a mo - ment;
Di - ane sit - tin' on
scratch - es his
D
E
A
Jack - y's lap. He's got his hands be - tween her knees.
head and does his best James Dean.

E
D
E
Jack, he says, "Hey, Di - ane, let's run off be - hind a shad - y tree;
"Well, then, there, Di - ane, we got - ta run off to the cit -
A
E
- y."
drib - ble off those Bob - bie Brooks. Let me
Di - ane says, "Ba - by, you ain't
D
E
A
A
E
do what I please."
miss - in' a thing."
Say - in',
But Jack, he says,
Oh yeah,
D
E
life goes on,

A
E
D
E
long af - ter the thrill of liv - ing is gone.
Say - in', oh yeah,
A
E
D
E
A
E
life goes on, long af - ter the
To Coda
1
D
E
A
thrill of liv - ing is gone. Now, walk on.

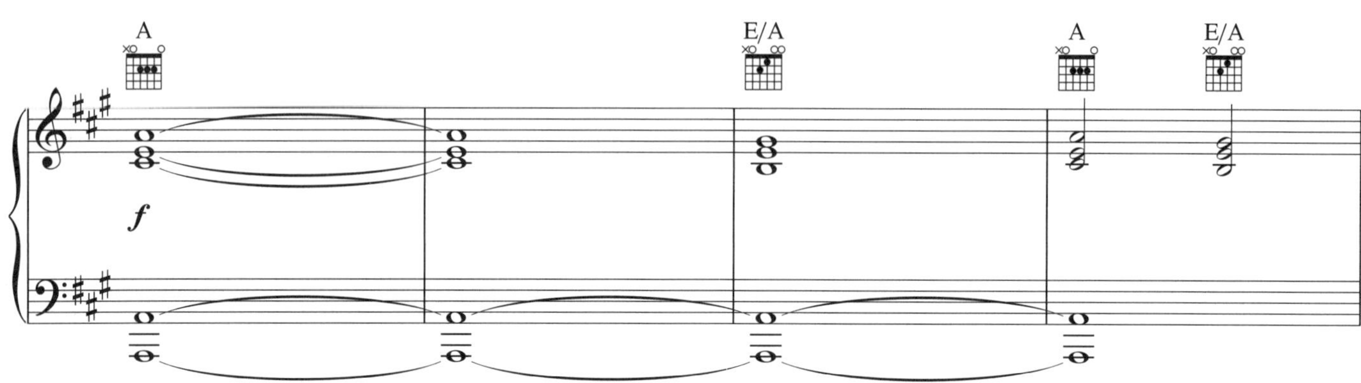
A
E/A
A
E/A
f

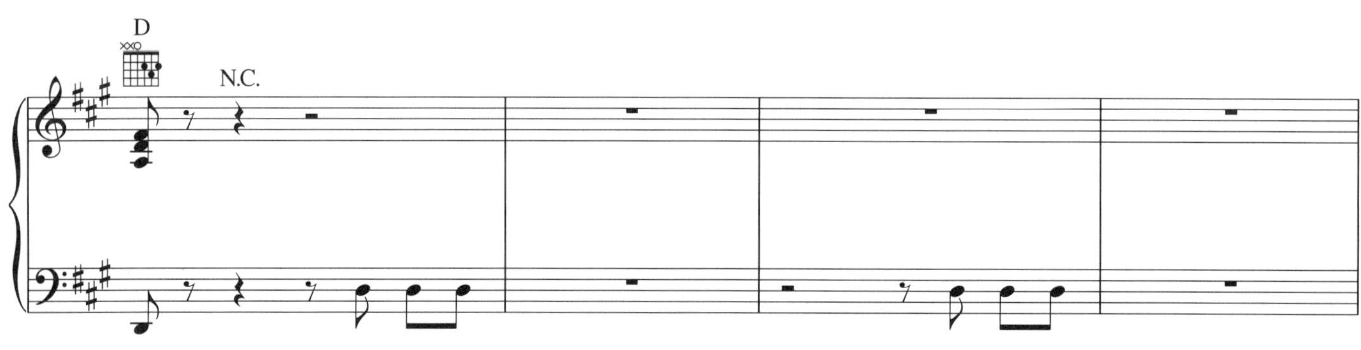
D
N.C.

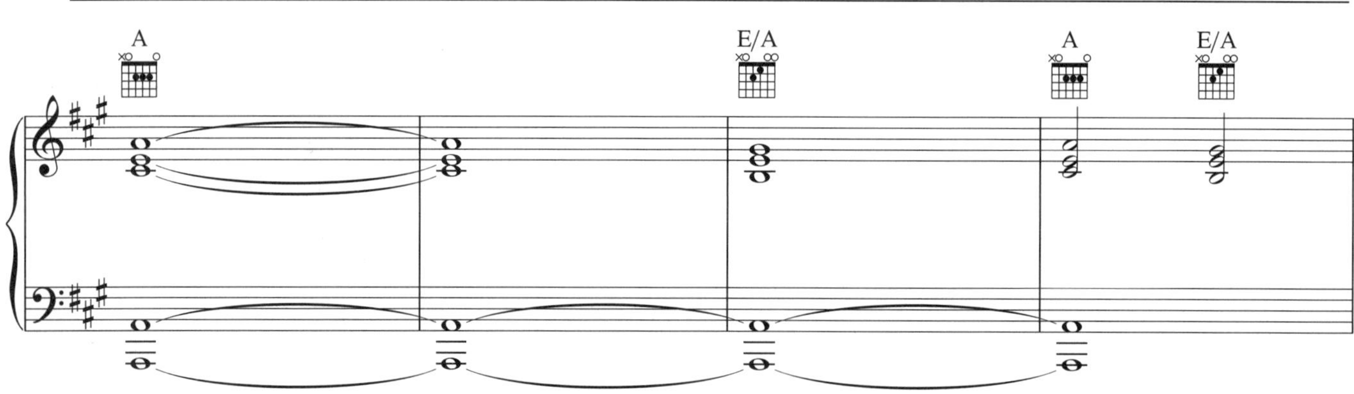
A
E/A
A
E/A

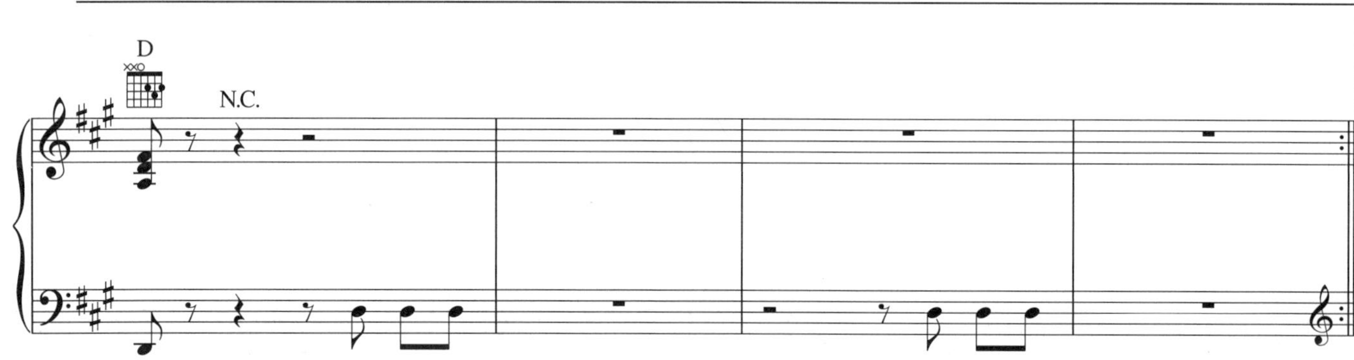
D
N.C.

2
N.C.
Oh, let it rock, let it roll,
let the Bi - ble Belt come and
save my soul.
Hold - in' on to
six - teen as long as you can;

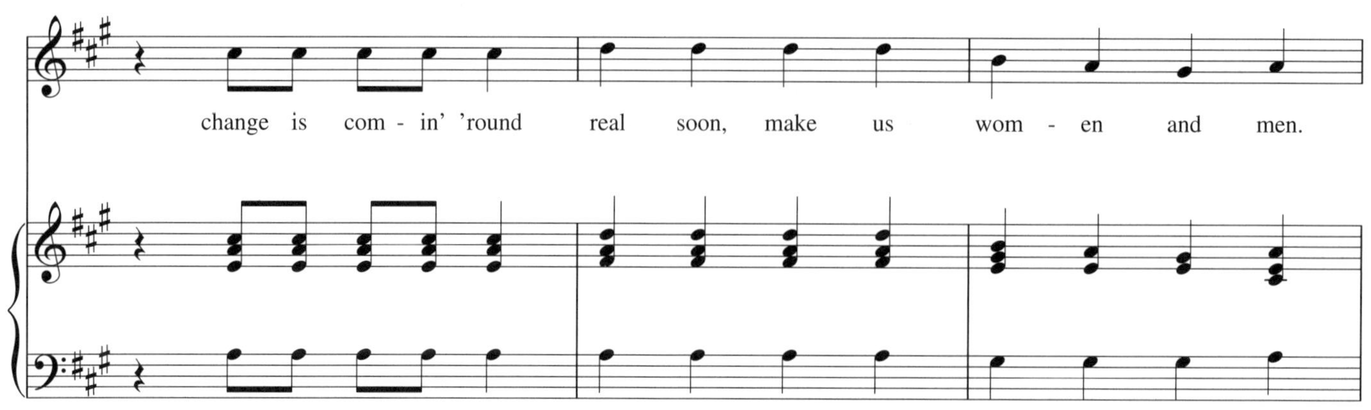
change is com - in' 'round real soon, make us wom - en and men.

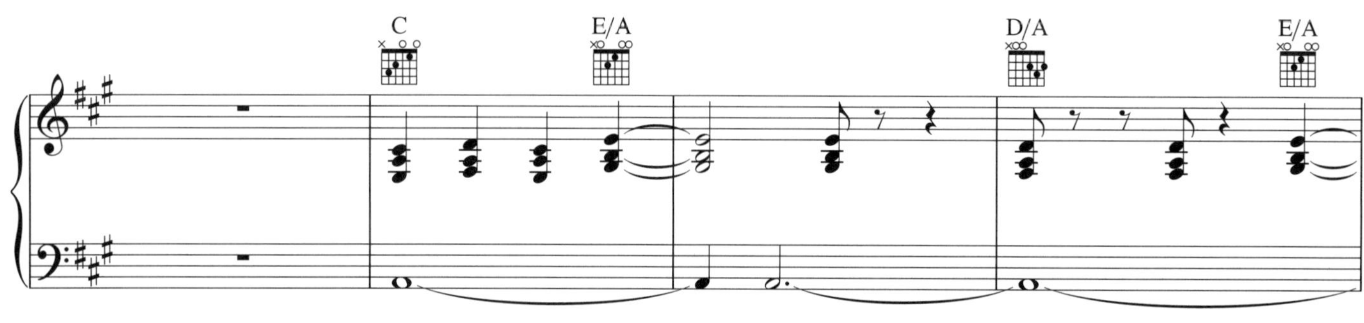
C
E/A
D/A
E/A

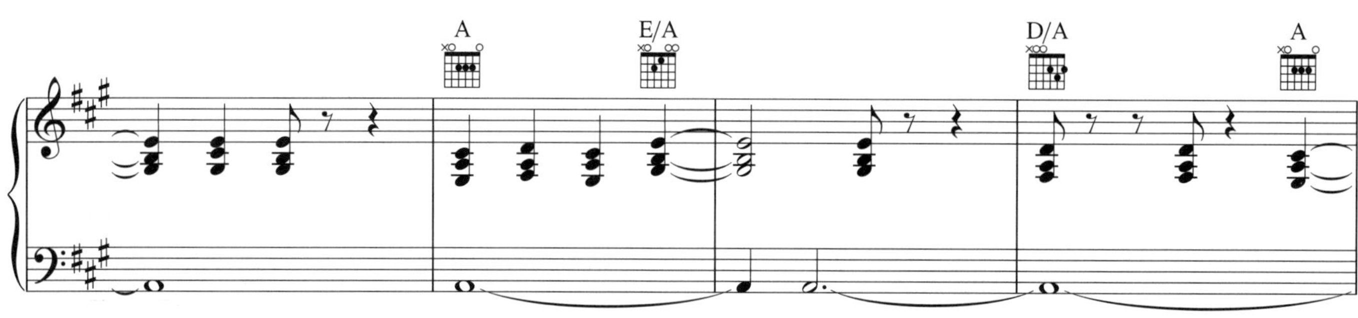
A
E/A
D/A
A

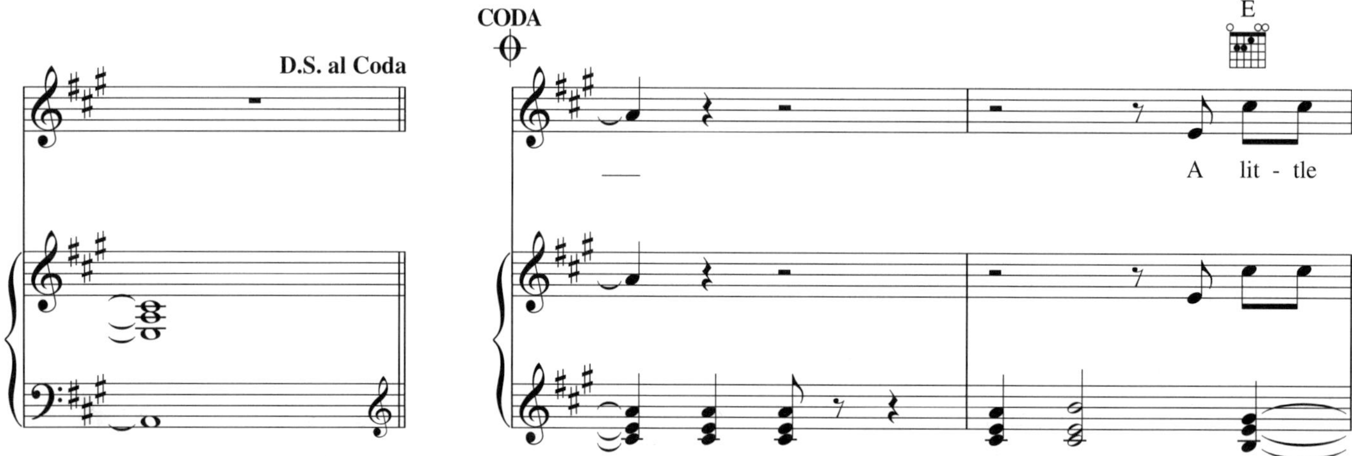
D.S. al Coda
CODA
E
A lit - tle

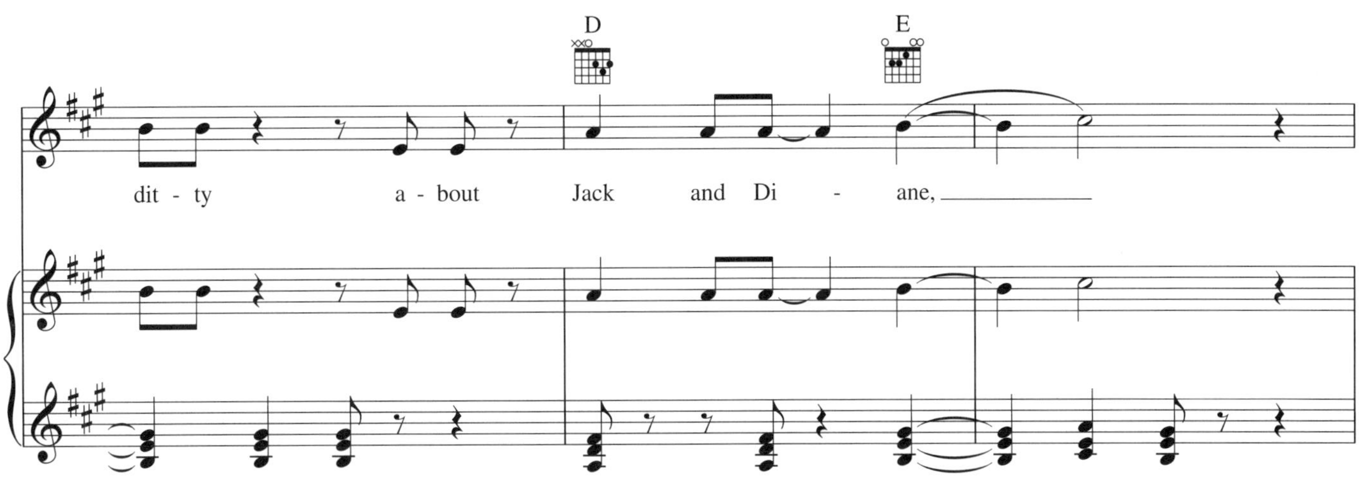
D
E
dit - ty a - bout Jack and Di - ane,

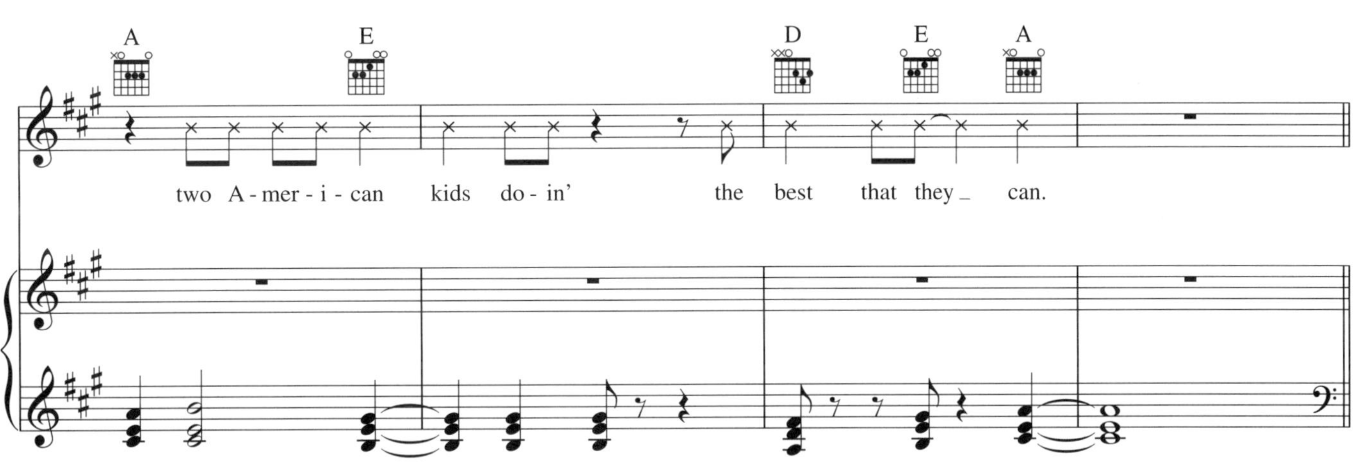
A
E
D
E
A
two A - mer - i - can kids do - in' the best that they can.

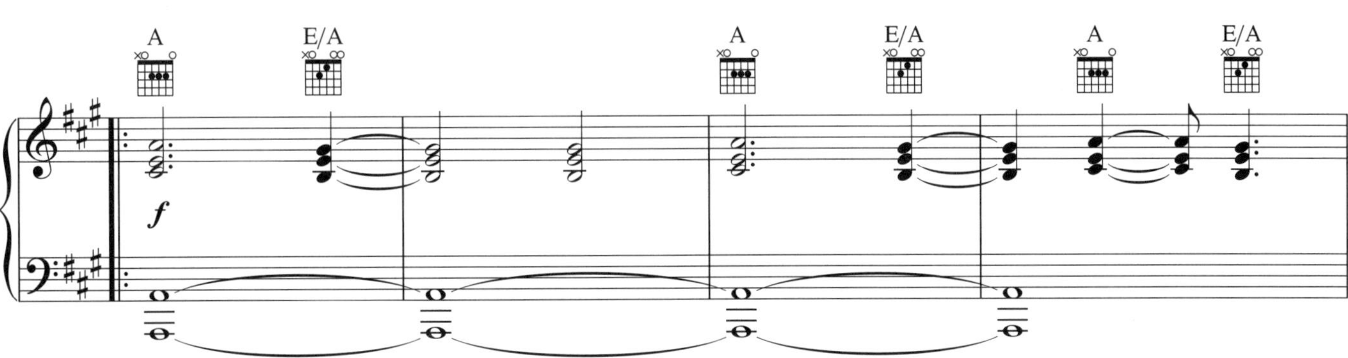
A
E/A
A
E/A
A
E/A
f

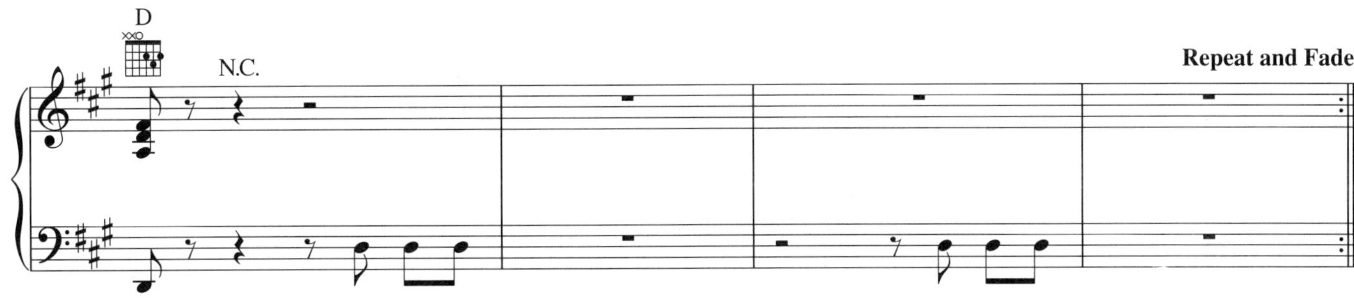
D
N.C.
Repeat and Fade

Imagine

Words and Music by John Lennon

Am/E
Dm7
F/C
G
C/G
I-mag-ine all the peo - ple
liv-ing for to-day.
G7
C
Cmaj7
F
Ah.
I-mag-ine there's no coun - tries.
sions.
C
Cmaj7
F
It is-n't hard to do.
I won-der if you can.
C
Cmaj7
F
Noth-ing to kill or die for,
No need for greed or hun - ger,

C
Cmaj7
F
and no re - li - gion, too.
a broth - er - hood of man.
Am/E
Dm7
F/C
I - mag - ine all the peo - ple
I - mag - ine all the peo - ple
G
C/G
G7
F
G
liv - ing life in peace.
shar - ing all the world.
You, you may say I'm a
C
E7
F
G
dream - er, but I'm not the on - ly one.

C
E7
F
G
I hope some - day you'll
join us
1
and the world will
be as one.
Cmaj7
I - mag - ine no pos - ses -
2
and the world will live as one.

Leader of the Band

Words and Music by Dan Fogelberg

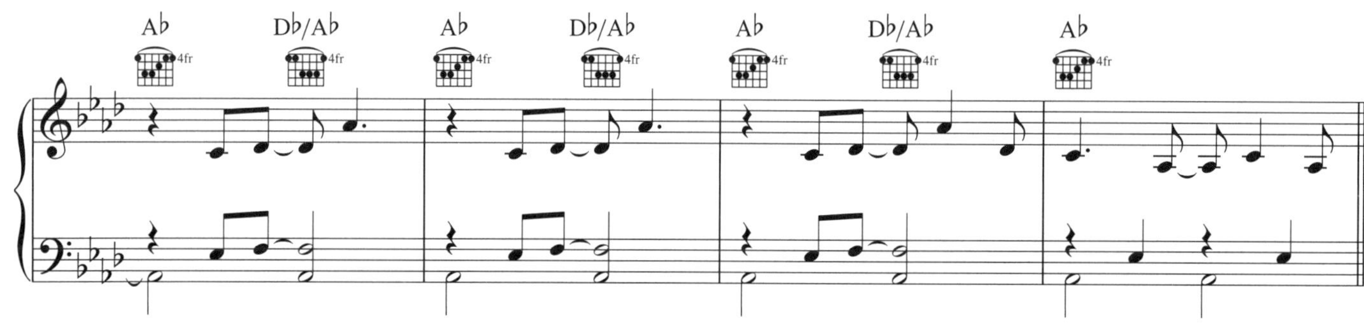

D♭
B♭m
Fm
his hands were meant for dif - f'rent work and his
he tried to be a sol - dier once but his
heart was known to none.
mu - sic would - n't wait.
E♭
A♭
D♭/A♭
He left his home and went
He earned his love through dis -
his lone and sol - i - tar - y way, and he
- ci - pline, a thun - d'ring vel - vet hand. His
Cm
3fr
4fr
gave to me a gift I know I nev - er can re -
gen - tle means of sculpt - ing souls took me years to un - der -
E♭7

1
A♭
D♭/A♭
A♭
D♭/A♭
A♭
D♭/A♭
A♭
pay.
2
A♭
D♭
Cm
stand. The lead - er of the band is tired and his
D♭
A♭
B♭m
eyes are grow - ing old, but his blood runs through my
Fm
B♭m
G♭
E♭
in - stru - ment and his song is in my soul.

D♭
Cm
D♭
My life has been a poor at - tempt to im - i - tate the man.
A♭
B♭m
Fm
B♭m
D♭
I'm just a liv - ing leg - a - cy to the lead - er of the
A♭
D♭/A♭
A♭
D♭/A♭
A♭
D♭/A♭
A♭
band.
A♭
D♭/A♭
A♭
Cm
D♭
My broth - er's lives were dif - f'rent for they heard an - oth - er call;
I thank you for the mu - sic and your sto - ries of the road.

B♭m
Fm
B♭m
one went to Chi - ca - go, and the oth - er to St.
I thank you for the free - dom when it came my time to
D♭
E♭
A♭
D♭/A♭
A♭
3fr
4fr
Paul. And I'm in Col - o - ra - do when I'm
go. I thank you for the kind - ness and the
Cm
D♭
B♭m
not in some ho - tel, liv - ing out this life
times when you got tough. And Pa - pa, I don't think
To Coda
Fm
B♭m
A♭
D♭/A♭
A♭
I've chose and come to know so well.
I said "I love you" near e -

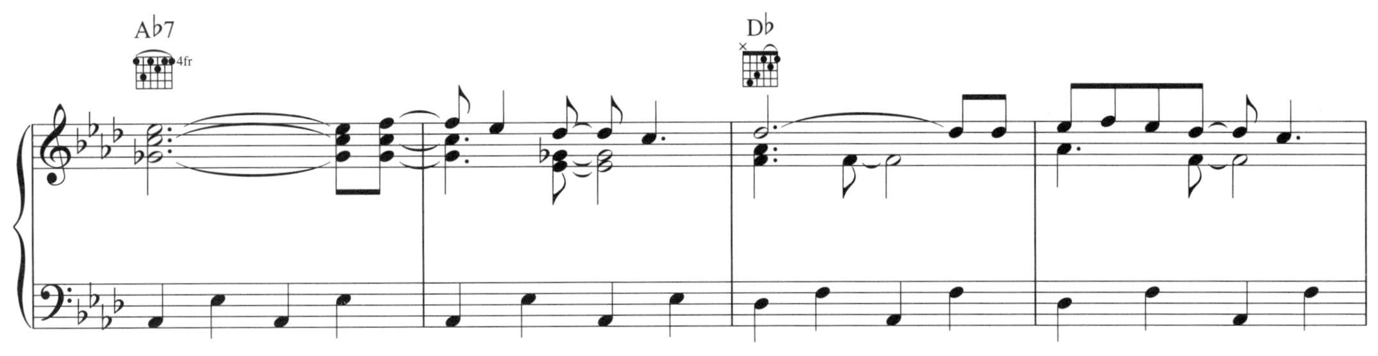
Ab7
4fr
Db

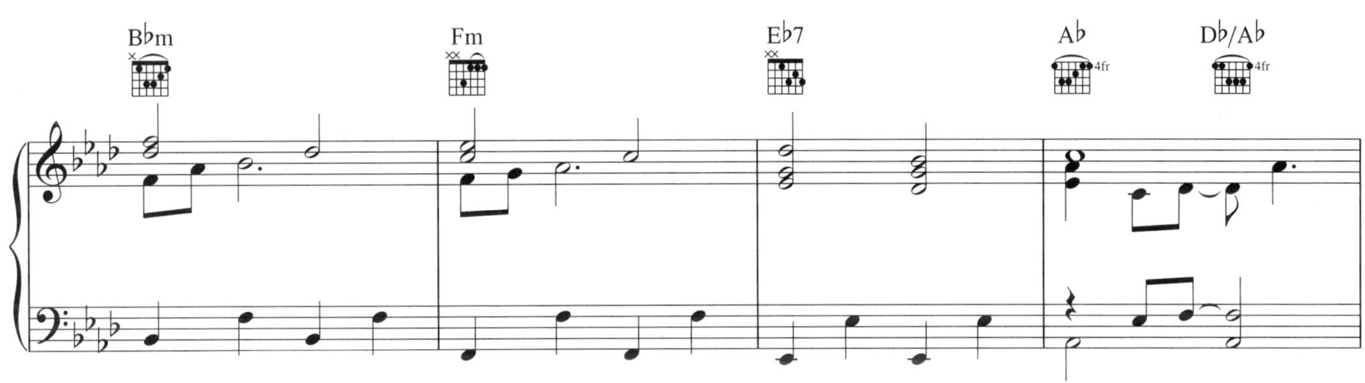
Bbm
Fm
Eb7
Ab
4fr
Db/Ab
4fr

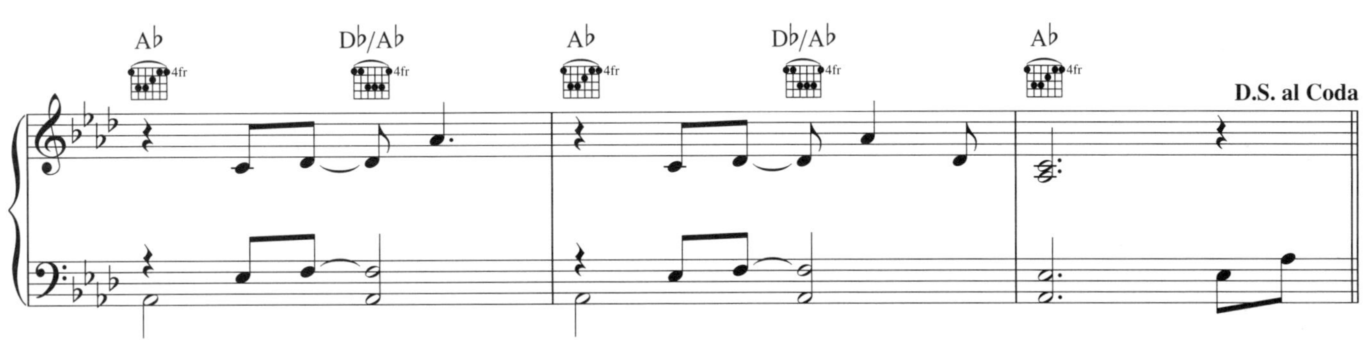
Ab
4fr
Db/Ab
4fr
Ab
4fr
Db/Ab
4fr
Ab
4fr
D.S. al Coda

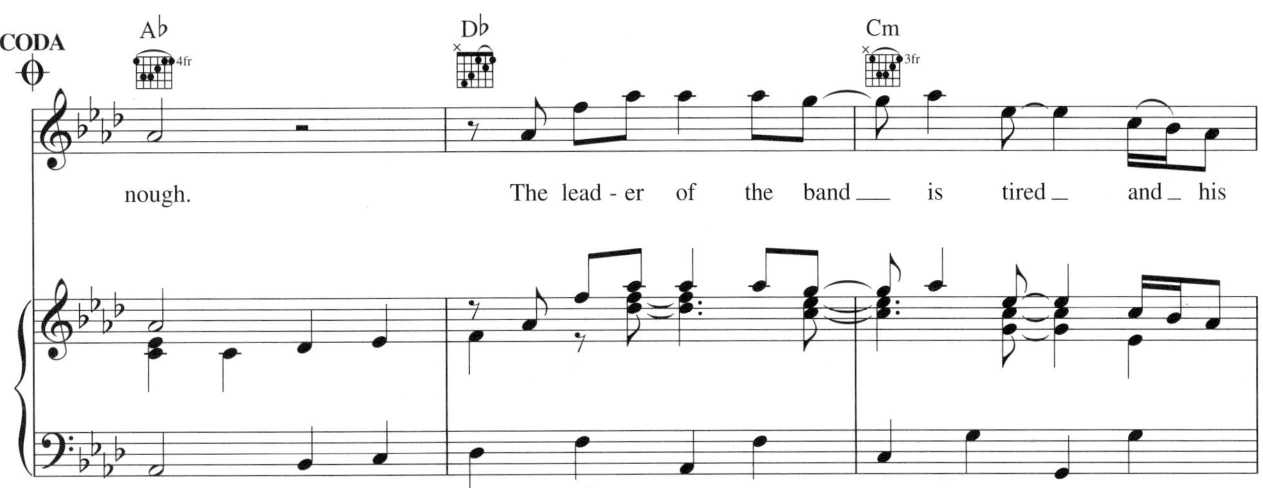
CODA
Ab
4fr
Db
Cm
3fr
nough.
The lead - er of the band is tired and his

D♭
A♭
4fr
B♭m
Fm
eyes are grow - ing old,
but his blood runs through my
in - stru - ment and his
B♭m
G♭
E♭
3fr
D♭
Cm
3fr
song is in my soul.
My life has been a poor at - tempt
D♭
A♭
4fr
B♭m
Fm
to im - i - tate the man.
I'm just a liv - ing leg - a - cy to the
B♭m
D♭
A♭
4fr
B♭m
lead - er of the band.
I am the liv - ing

Fm
Bbm
Db
Eb
3fr
leg - a - cy to the lead - er of the
Ab
4fr
Db/Ab
band.
Ab7
Bbm
Fm
Eb7

Leaving on a Jet Plane

Words and Music by John Denver

G
C
G
dawn is break - in', it's ear - ly morn. The taxi - i's wait - in', he's
place I go I'll think of you. Ev - 'ry song I sing I'll
Dream a - bout the days to come, when I won't have to
C
G
C
blow - in' his horn. Al - read - y I'm so lone - some I could
sing for you. When I come back I'll bring wear your wed - ding
leave a - lone. A - bout the times I won't have to
D
G
C
die.
ring.
say:
So kiss me and smile for me.
G
C
G
Am
Tell me that you'll wait for me. Hold me like you'll nev - er let me go.

D7
G
C
'Cause I'm leav - in' on a jet plane;
G
C
D7
G
C
don't know when I'll be back a - gain. Oh babe, I hate to
1, 2
D7
C/D
3
D7
go. There's so go. 'Cause I'm
Repeat and Fade
G
C
G
C
D7
leav - in'
Leav - in'
on a jet plane; don't know when I'll be back a - gain.

Performance Notes

Amanda *(page 6)*

Boston's guitarist, songwriter, and geeky rock guru Tom Scholz, an MIT grad and, at one time, an engineer for Polaroid, has been famous from the outset for his extreme meticulousness in the studio. Scholz's attention to detail paid off when the band's first album, *Boston* (1976), became the biggest selling debut album at the time, eclipsed only by Whitney Houston's debut ten years later. Scholz and company released their second album, begrudgingly and under relentless pressure from their record company, just two years later. That album, *Don't Look Back,* also went to the top of the charts and sold fairly well, but Scholz himself couldn't stand it. In fact, he was so disappointed with the effort that he swore never to work on anyone else's timetable again. Seven years and 12,000 hours of studio time later, Boston released its *next* album, *Third Stage,* a recording led by this song, "Amanda." Coming as it did between the vinyl and CD formats, *Third Stage* was the first album to go gold on both record and CD, thanks in large part to "Amanda," the band's only #1 hit single. Written six years before its release, "Amanda" also ended up being one of the few post-MTV songs that reached #1 on the charts without a video.

A standard key (G) and 4/4 time make "Amanda" a rock-solid classic. The key of G has one sharp (F♯), right there in the staff. 4/4 means you count four quarter notes in each measure. But don't let this beauty's simplicity fool you. You're playing a true classic.

Keep it slow, daddy-o, but don't lose the cool accent. Pretend you're the drummer. Find something solid to tap four beats on. While repeating it, accent the first and third beats. *One,* two, *three,* four / *one,* two, *three,* four. That's the rhythmic essence of "Amanda."

Save time now by looking ahead to bar 48, right after the lyric, "Oh, Girl." Become familiar with those few measures containing several G♯ notes you wouldn't find in the key of G. Don't fret, it's not as painful as a bad guitar pun and lasts less than a page. Just avoid the surprise there by playing through the section a couple of times.

American Pie *(page 14)*

"American Pie" hit the American cultural consciousness in 1972 and sold upwards of three million copies. But the real magic of McLean's rock hymn is its ambitious and ambiguous themes. We can never clearly define all the images and allusions he refers to; like in good poetry, they are left to interpretation. McLean's verses resonate with emotion and we clearly understand that the songwriter, and the entire country, lost something significant, but what, exactly? Rock and roll? Peace? Innocence? Optimism? McLean himself has stayed relatively mum about the song's true meaning, choosing only to describe it in an interview as "a story about America."

The full version of "American Pie" ran eight and a half minutes long and occupied both sides of a 45 rpm, the most common format at the time. Because of that minor inconvenience, the song needed to be flipped by DJs that wanted to play the whole record, and most did not. Still, it climbed to #1 a few weeks after its release. When McLean first performed the song in public in 1970, he didn't know the lyrics well enough to sing them from memory, so he asked a young woman from the audience to turn his lyrics sheet pages for him. You might have to do this too, if you're tempted to sing the entire song while playing!

This musical feast features many *rolled chords,* marked by a curved line beside them. Locate the lyric: "But February made me shiver . . ." and play the rolled chords quickly from bottom to top. Try the *sustain pedal* (the pedal you find on the far right) to help the notes ring out. However, be sure to lift the pedal between rolls to keep this confection crisp and sweet!

Know your patterns. This epic tale mesmerizes us with repeating patterns. By familiarizing yourself, new parts seem easy already. A great example is the chorus. The repeating lower notes reappear many times throughout. So, take an extra minute, play them, and let your finger memory take charge. Look for more now, or play on with abandon.

At Seventeen (page 24)

Most casual pop fans that recall Janis Ian's hit "At Seventeen" don't realize she actually debuted at 12. The precocious New York City teen, born Janis Eddy Fink — Ian was her brother's middle name — was a bona fide child prodigy, turning heads early on with hits "Society's Child" and "Hair of Spun Gold." By the time she was 14, smack in the middle of the 1960s, she was taking blues and acoustic guitar lessons from the legendary Reverend Gary Davis. Her notoriety secured her gigs in Greenwich Village's active and influential folk scene.

Janis survived the '60s. She battled her record company around every turn, trying desperately to overcome her "child prodigy" tag and attempting to exist on her own, making her own career decisions. She did encounter many more troubles along the way though, including several attempts on her life, a cocaine binge with Jimi Hendrix, an investigation by the FBI, and other colorful escapades. On the plus side, she appeared on *Saturday Night Live's* debut episode as the series' first musical guest, and she won a bunch of GRAMMY® awards, including one for the song listed here.

The hushed and chilling "At Seventeen," is a prototype of Ian's intimate, confessional style. From very early on, she wrote from a deeply personal place, and her arresting candor helped her build a sizable fan base quickly. A literate and heartfelt writer, Ian spoke her mind in what was then referred to by her record company as "anti-parent music."

Keep this thoughtful journey on the slow road. *Moderately,* derived from the Italian term, *moderato,* indicates a moderate tempo, but don't play it too relaxed or mellow! Strong emotion fills this ballad of teen angst.

Blackbird (page 28)

Anything that appeared on The Beatles' so-called *White Album* — okay, on any of their albums — has been enshrined in the pantheon of pop music for all time, and so discussion becomes moot. We love them. We love their songs. Everything that could be written about them and much more has already been committed to paper. That's pretty much the end of the story.

But that doesn't solve the problem of this entry, which must be written, and must include something at least moderately interesting. Hmmm . . . Did you know that . . . Um, that one's too obvious. I had heard that when Paul and John were writing songs for . . . No, not that either. That's unsubstantiated. How about this: Paul McCartney, the writer of the song, recorded it himself in the studio alone with an acoustic guitar accompaniment. And for a long time, the song remained a solo performance. Eventually they added a second acoustic guitar accompaniment and tacked on those cute bird sound effects at the end.

Be an early bird by mastering the five-note rhythm that appears early and often. Find it in the second measure. The theme is played twice there, in the lower staff. The trick is to count five notes in two beats. Try it (one-and-a), then count beat 2 as *two and.* But remember, that *two and* must occupy only one beat. So you count it: one *(and-a)* two and. Repeat that a few times and you'll soon be winging through this beauty.

Note how the time signature moves freely between 2/4, 3/4, and 4/4. All rhythms are based on quarter notes, hence the bottom number: 4. The top number (2, 3, or 4) tells you how many quarter notes per measure. In each measure, try to *feel* each of those beats! All else (the tempo, the key, and so on) stays the same, so no need to squawk when you see the change!

Take a minute to scout out the sharps and flats in "Blackbird." Although written in the key of G (which contains F♯), The Beatles use *accidentals* (sharps, flats, and naturals written alongside the notes). A quick scan and you'll be ready to play, like The Beatles did, simply yet classically!

Candle in the Wind (page 32)

We could very easily get serious here, and talk about how this song is a powerful rumination on the cult of celebrity. Elton and his lyricist Bernie Taupin originally composed these lyrics to address the sad, early death of Marilyn Monroe. And of course, they were rewritten to address Princess Diana as well in 1997, when they changed the lyrics from "goodbye Norma Jean" to "goodbye England's rose," for Diana's funeral. But although the subject matter has a certain morose relevance, the melody is more graceful than dour, more elegant than funereal. Oddly enough, the recording was never officially released as a single in the United States. When DJs first received the music from Elton's label, they chose to play the flip side, "Bennie and the Jets," and not Elton's intended single. No matter. Over the years, the song grew in stature within Elton's catalog and is now one of his most beloved tunes. It builds beautifully, with a gentle but insistent dynamic, until the singer himself releases his tightly wound heart with a wail of cathartic and quite tragic longing.

Although the piece is marked *Gently, reflectively,* don't go too easy on the piano part. Elton John uses the dynamic power of the keyboard to express emotion in this masterpiece. He and Billy Joel triumphed with the rock piano style, carrying and passing along the torch lit by Jerry Lee Lewis, Little Richard, and so many other early great keyboard artists.

Rock that piano, not literally, but with an accent on the *offbeat.* Rock and roll puts an accent on *three* (the third beat, or offbeat), creating a rocking sensation. Prior to the advent of rock and roll, 4/4 beats took their cue from marching bands, where a strong first beat kept all in step, on the *downbeat.* Though subtle for this flickering candle, an offbeat still hints at the rocking motion that keeps the heart of rock and roll beating.

Change the World (page 46)

Eric Clapton has always had a heavy romantic streak, starting way back. Early songs like "Layla" and "Bell-Bottom Blues" were prototypical rock star love ditties, and, of course, there's always "Wonderful Tonight," a prom-date favorite for all eternity. "Change the World" falls in line with those tunes, though not as melodically timeless and lyrically touching. Clapton swings for the fence on this one, singing about reaching for the stars, being the sunlight in her universe, and, yes, wondering what it would be like to be king for a day. (Don't we all?)

Despite its lyrical over-reach, the public ate it up after the song first appeared in the 1996 movie, *Phenomenon.* The tune earned multiple GRAMMYs for song, record, and male pop vocal, and was selected by the Recording Industry Association of America as one of the Songs of the Century, slotted on the chart at #271.

Learn to love the key of E. E major is a wonderful key to master! Start by finding the four sharps and play them once. They are F♯, C♯, G♯, and D♯. Close your eyes and enjoy the sweet sound! E major has a rich sound, and is a favorite of many singers.

Be a quick learner by finding *dotted notes* and *tied notes* in the first line of "Change the World." Notes with a dot right after them get an extra half beat. For *tied notes*, find the notes *tied* into the second measure. Notes tied together are held as one note, meaning they aren't played again, but just held down. Congratulate yourself for time well spent. You've learned a lot. To prove this, find the many dotted and tied notes throughout and relish Clapton's soaring feelings.

Don't avoid *accidentals* in this moving vehicle. Accidentals are *sharps, flats,* or *naturals* written beside a note that aren't part of the key signature. Be sure to catch these accidentals as you play. If you ignore them, many jazz and blues notes are dropped; including them is worth the extra effort.

Crazy Little Thing Called Love (page 39)

Starting in the late 1970s, pop music began evolving into a more electronic and dance-oriented creation. Queen had emerged from a hit-making run throughout the decade characterized by the amazing "Bohemian Rhapsody." In 1980, Queen began making wholesale changes to their sound, in part to keep things fresh, but also to keep up with the times. They journeyed to Munich, Germany, a figurative and literal departure for the band, to record their new album, appropriately titled, *The Game.* They had previously insisted on recording in the United Kingdom, with longtime producer Roy Thomas Baker. But for *The Game* they set up shop in Germany and used synthesizers for the very first time.

Of course, this didn't bother the legions of Queen fans, all of whom were thrilled by the danceability of the album's singles, including this and the equally huge "Another One Bites the Dust." Powered by these Queen classics, *The Game* rose to #1 on the charts. More impressively, *The Game* was the only album to ever top the *Billboard* Rock, Dance, and R&B charts at the same time. As for this song, lore has it that Freddie Mercury, Queen's beloved singer, wrote it while lounging in a bubble bath at the Munich Bayerischerhof Hotel, which, knowing Freddie, doesn't surprise us at all!

This tune is aptly described as a moderately *fast shuffle,* because it gets folks moving, dancing, or at least tapping their toes! Now put a little accent on beats 2 and 4 (as opposed to 1 and 3) for a feeling of "jumpin' jive!" You might call this key "C with a twist." With no sharps or flats in the key signature many *accidentals* (sharps and flats written next to the notes) soon appear. The composer, Freddie Mercury, spices up the key of C by plugging in notes from closely related keys. This is the sign of a bright, inventive, and in our opinion, highly underrated songwriter. Hardly a "crazy little song," those sharps and flats show the wit of a master.

Vamp on it a couple of times for the full effect! You can repeat the entire first measure two extra times (or even longer) without losing the beat. This practice of *vamping* (repeating a phrase) comes from theater, where an orchestra waits for the singer to begin. Catchy introductions evolved, where an extra measure would get the party started!

Don't Let the Sun Go Down on Me (page 52)

Anyone over age 40 knows that Elton John was on fire in the 1970s, with more smash tunes and hit albums than just about anybody else. What The Beatles were to the '60s, Elton was to the '70s. To wit, in 1992, Reginald Kenneth Dwight (his real name) broke Elvis Presley's record for the most consecutive years of Top 40 hits on *Billboard's* singles chart, having placed a song on the chart every year since debuting with "Your Song" back in December of 1970. In a three-year span from 1973 to 1976 Elton dominated with fifteen hit songs, including six #1 hits ("Crocodile Rock," "Bennie and the Jets," "Lucy in the Sky with Diamonds," "Philadelphia Freedom," "Island Girl," and "Don't Go Breaking My Heart"), and three that reached #2 ("Daniel," "Goodbye Yellow Brick Road," and "Don't Let the Sun Go Down on Me").

Of his many memorable tunes, "Don't Let the Sun Go Down on Me" might be the song we remember most fondly. Bernie Taupin, Elton's songwriting partner, came up with some tender, winning lyrics that Elton really lays into in his inimitable way. In 1992, almost 20 years later, John re-recorded the song as a live duet with George Michael, and, like a Roman candle, it soared to #2. Some things you just can't keep down, like this masterpiece from the bespectacled one.

Start quietly! This sun takes its time going down before the *chorus* stops the sands of time. At the line, "Don't let the sun go down on me. . . ," we wonder if it may be a sunrise instead. So wait patiently, softly building the volume until that point. Then let it all hang out!

Sixteenth notes abound in this classic. Don't forget that four sixteenth notes make one beat in 4/4 time. Locate the last four notes of the very first measure. Those four notes equal only one beat, so keep those fingers nimble.

Dust in the Wind (page 64)

Like many of the best so-called "progressive" bands — Yes, Genesis, and Emerson, Lake & Palmer to name just a few — Kansas was able to leaven its far-reaching musical aspirations with good solid songcraft. Their most memorable tunes, like "Carry On Wayward Son" and "Point of No Return," had a melodic core wrapped in magical instrumental challenges. "Dust in the Wind" is unusual because it's the band's first foray into acoustic songwriting. Although some believe the guitar track is a twelve-string acoustic, it's actually two six-strings playing simultaneously.

"Dust in the Wind," is songwriter Kerry Livgren's philosophical knockout punch, a simple yet sublime sentiment that Kansas pondered in its journey to become true rock and roll superstars. Interestingly, Livgren came out with this pop psychology nugget just as the band was cresting in popularity. At the time, he was reading a book of Native American literature, which profoundly affected his outlook. He was also grappling with the idea of becoming larger than life as a mega-rock star and how it conflicted with thoughts of his own mortality. In other words, he'd soon be "dust in the wind" like everybody else.

Play that folkie music! You are directed to adopt a *Moderate Folk style,* so give a smooth, mellow feel to this classic. Try to reproduce a guitar fingerpicking sound by letting one note glide into the next. Use the *sustain pedal* (the pedal on the far right) to let the notes ring out and fade gently, as they would on a guitar. This ballad is far from void of emotion, so keep a solid, soft intensity.

Voicing is deciding how loud to make each note. When you reach the solo on the fourth page, those notes must ring louder than the rest! *Melody* notes (the notes the singer sings), likewise, are voiced louder than *accompanying* tones beneath. Look at the first lyric, "I close my eyes." That melody must stand out. Hint: The top notes in the piano are almost always the melody. But if in doubt, quickly check the lyric line. Once you find your voice, let it sing.

Free Fallin' (page 70)

In 1987, an arsonist set fire to the Petty family home. At the time, Petty was on a creative high, having just come off working with the Traveling Wilburys and its luminous lineup. He'd also started work on his own album, *Full Moon Fever.* When the fire struck, his family, while unharmed, lost virtually everything it owned. The devastation left the Pettys in a weird sort of limbo. They bopped from home to home until they found a permanent residence. While he admits it was an unsettled lifestyle, his nomadic existence proved to be a boon for his songwriting.

The first two singles off the album, "I Won't Back Down" and "Runnin' from a Dream," did well. Both songs helped Petty work through his frustrations in a therapeutic way. But it was "Free Fallin'" that struck a major chord with pop audiences, and its success helped *Full Moon Fever* surpass *Damn the Torpedoes* as the band's best selling album.

Fall into fun. Keep this one peppy and not a downer. Begin by tapping your foot to keep the rhythm steady so you don't lose the beat. The sustained notes have an intensity that is the driving force behind this ride.

Expect the unexpected on your first play-through. The tune uses many *suspended chords.* A suspended chord has a rogue note (or two) that isn't usually there. For example, the opening stacked notes are C, F, and A. These notes make up a major F chord and sound fine together. The next notes are C, F, and B♭. That B♭ sounds weird in there, *suspended* between A and C, wanting to *resolve* to one or the other. It creates the mood of the song, suspended in air, free-falling.

Jazz up the solo a little! Unless you're playing with other instruments, consider trying to express yourself a little in the solo section. The original recording features drums there. So if you're creative and know how to improvise a bit (or someone can show you how), add a little flair. If not, don't worry. It's fine to be played as written!

Give a Little Bit (page 59)

In the rock-star-rich 1970s, production budgets for albums were sky-high, even for an unassuming British band like Supertramp. In the mid-70s, the band journeyed to the Rocky Mountains of Colorado, to begin recording an album at Caribou Ranch studios just outside of Denver. Little did they know that the rare air at that elevation did bizarre things to recorded music. For one, it made singing difficult; notes wavered and vibrato went in crazy directions. It also made John Helliwell's saxophones sound strangely off key. Who knew? But it didn't take the band long to head west to L.A. to finish recording.

Despite its "rocky" origins, *Even in the Quietest Moments* was Supertramp's most popular work until their epic *Breakfast in America* was released. "Give a Little Bit" became the band's first Top 20 hit in the U.S. and Supertramp's first gold record as well. It was the opening salvo of the quirky band's hit parade, which continued with "The Logical Song," "Goodbye Stranger," and, of course, "Take the Long Way Home."

D may be a lousy grade but it's sure an excellent key. Note the sharps signs (♯) on the staff. That's called the *key signature*. Both staves have an F♯ and C♯ in them, meaning the key of D.

This one is easy as one, two, three . . . um, I mean four! In 4/4, each measure contains exactly four beats, each beat being a quarter note long. So a quarter note takes up one beat. See, four can be easy as three.

Have You Ever Seen the Rain? (page 74)

1970 was a rough year. The peace, love, and understanding ballyhooed by the hippies at Woodstock went up in a puff of marijuana smoke when some Hell's Angels snuffed out a concert-goer at Altamont, another festival. And the Vietnam War began to seem never-ending. At John Fogerty's Creedence Clearwater Revival headquarters, things weren't so good either. He and his brother Tom weren't getting along. Their musical relationship was complicated. The younger John played in Tom's band in the early '60s. Then they formed another band in which they shared lead singing and songwriting equally. Finally, in CCR, John became the leader, and almost all of Tom's work for John was cast aside. Needless to say, this created serious strain on the Fogerty boys' fraternal order and the animosity led Tom to quit the band in 1971.

One of the only benefits of all of this turbulence was John's song, "Have You Ever Seen the Rain?" Its opening line, "Someone told me long ago, there's a calm before the storm, I know, it's been coming for some time," poetically documented what had to have been a very difficult time for the family. Tom went on to make four solo albums, three of which were issued before his death in 1990, and one that saw a posthumous release.

Hum that *bass line*. People do recognize and hum those lower notes. Play through the first measures or bars with the left hand here. That basic *riff* is laid out there, before the lyrics even start, so no need to ask if anyone's seen it!

Check out the fine *suspended (sus)* chord technique on the third page of this jewel. On the lyrics "comin' down" the chords move from F to G, but the melody hangs on to C, part of the F chord. That C is the *suspended note*. It is suspended while the tune moves, creating that great rock and roll signature sound!

Balance the *accents* here. The bass comes in on the first beat, normally the most accented in 4/4 time. But the *melody* (singing) starts on the second beat, giving it an accent too. So, let your hands work together trading it off, giving equal accents to both beats one and two.

Honesty (page 78)

So you want to tackle a tune by the "Piano Man"? A good place to start is his album *52nd Street,* a 1978 recording that boasts three super-huge hits: "Honesty," the more aggressive "Big Shot," and "My Life." Joel, in typical New York fashion, tends to take the cynical side of the argument. On "Big Shot," he takes down a nemesis with some finely pointed name-calling. "Honesty" is actually a plea for truth in romantic relationships. "Tenderness is easy to find," he writes, but "you search for truthfulness, you might just as well be blind." And this was before old Billy got all mixed up with trophy wives!

In truth, for quite some time early in his career Joel had suffered setbacks, both in his career and in his love life, all of which amounted to a bout of severe depression. When he was just 21 years old, Billy ended up in the psychiatric ward of a Long Island hospital for a few weeks. "You couldn't leave," he said to *Rolling Stone.* "You're in the snake pit." And so he vowed at that point to never again think he couldn't resolve his own problems.

The key of B♭ brings a truly bright flavor to this lovely ode. The *key signature,* located where the staff begins, indicates B♭ and E♭. So, whenever you see a B or E, play the note a half step below. A key signature is a golden gift, making the page less cluttered and easier to read!

Keep that left hand jumpin'! The marking L.H. appears under the notes in the third measure, which means the left hand plays them. The right hand does tickle that single melody ivory line up top (find that upper B♭ in the melody line). Then do the rest as written. The connecting lines illustrate the jumps.

It's not a shocking truth, just a quirky lower bass line. That opening walk down, B♭, A♭, G♭, F, in the opening measures, is a beautiful yet unexpected progression, with two flats written that are not normally found in the key of B♭. Those notes ring out with surprising transcendence, just like "honesty."

I'll Follow the Sun (page 83)

Paul McCartney wrote this innocent little ditty in 1959 when he was just 16. At the time, he and John were in the band the Quarrymen, and they were feeling their oats as young musicians. "I wrote 'I'll Follow the Sun' in my front parlor in Forthlin Road," McCartney said in an interview with Beatles scholar Mark Lewisohn. "I seem to remember writing it just after I'd had the flu . . . I remember standing in the parlor, with my guitar, looking out through the lace curtains of the window, and writing that one."

Even though Sir Paul didn't think the song measured up to the standards of the band, the tune still followed The Beatles around. A rough home demo of the song, without the delicate arrangement of the final version, exists from the spring of 1960 featuring McCartney, John Lennon, and George Harrison (all on acoustic guitars), and then-bassist Stu Sutcliffe.

The song was revived during the rushed recording sessions for the album *Beatles for Sale* at the end of 1964. John, Paul, George, and Ringo recorded "I'll Follow the Sun" in eight takes, with the final version the only one to include electric guitar.

Do follow the bouncing ballad. Although the direction reads *moderately*, this beat should put a skip in your step. *Dotted notes* get an extra half beat. If followed by an eighth note, as in this Beatles' favorite, you'll feel a little jump! Find the many examples. The first happens in the opening lyric: "One day . . . "

Don't trip and lose your step by fumbling for notes. Those two chords in the right hand below the opening lyric, "One day," contain the same notes: G, B, and D. However, the order is different, because the bottom, or *root note,* changes! That second chord is called an *inversion.* Finding those notes quickly means more time to follow your heart and the sun.

If You Leave Me Now (page 86)

Long noted as a versatile act, capable of shuffling between R&B, rock, pop, Irish music, jazz, and blues, the Chicago lineup featured a canny combo of instrumental dexterity, gutsy performance, and pop savvy. In the fall of 1975, along comes the band's tenth album, unsurprisingly titled *Chicago X*, a disc that included the smash ballad, "If You Leave Me Now." Well, lots of people liked that song, and the album went double platinum in no time, based largely on the crossover/commercial success of this single.

The band had never seen such success. The song became Chicago's first #1 hit, and won a GRAMMY award for Record of the Year. They had hit on something big, and the band's management wanted more and more of the same. Peter Cetera, one of the band's principal writers and the singer of this song, began pumping out romantic ballads, like "Baby, What a Big Surprise" and "No Tell Lover."

Problem was, these romantic slow-dancers didn't excite the band much. It downplayed their musicianship, put the focus too much on Cetera, and ticked off their old fans. Still, this is not to say these songs were inferior. Who can forget swaying to the music to "If You Leave Me Now" at the school dance? Learning to play it will no doubt bring you back to those carefree, bell-bottomed days.

Jazz up your life with this Peter Cetera classic. The opening measure contains a C bass with a G chord above it. Jazz-influenced tunes can test an ear at first, but don't freak out. Once you put it all together, the notes sound fine and even sweet. It's simply a little musical tension to portray the jitters of a rocky romance.

It takes two. . . beats that is, here in 2/4 time, to make a point. The predominant time signature for the piece is 4/4, but changes several times, to 2/4 — which contains two beats instead of four. Locate the 2/4 sections and play those, adding a little extra accent and passion. The tempo stays the same. The big difference is that 2/4 measures last only half as long as the 4/4 measures.

Don't be left behind by the adventurous section on the second page! That melodic bridge which begins "A love like ours" contains a flurry of flats, so prime your fingers with a quick run through.

Imagine (page 100)

Ah, so here we are, making a stop at one of the world's best songs, written by none other than . . . Yoko Ono? What? Actually, don't laugh, because this is more feasible than you think, and at the very least many in the know feel that it absolutely should have been a Lennon/Ono byline.

Released in September 1971 in America and a month later in the UK, the title track of Lennon's *Imagine* was originally inspired by Ono. She says she often played the "imagine" game with her brother to picture a better world while growing up during World War II. She described how as a 12 year old, she'd use the power of imagination to visualize a more peaceful world as her own country, Japan, was bombed. Hungry and scared, they played the game in an attempt to transport each other to a happier, safer place. Much of this information, and some of the actual lyrics to "John's" song can be found in Ono's 1970 book, *Grapefruit.*

Certainly, John took great care in putting some of Yoko's words to music. It is the very simplicity of the sentiments expressed that makes the song so universal. And perhaps it's a sad indictment of our country that this song remains so significant. "Imagine" a period in our future in which we *wouldn't* be moved to tears when we heard this song. Then we'd be talking about a special time indeed.

You're not imagining those two bass clefs at the beginning of the piece. The opening music employs double bass clefs (also called F Clefs). So read both staves in bass clef, but don't miss the G clef when it does appear, right before the lyric "Imagine."

Nail that signature riff at the end of the second measure. That little *motif* A-A♯-B, in the piano part has become a musical icon, well-known to millions, so you'll want to be familiar with it. Find the best method to get your fingers around it so it keeps bringing hope and love to many!

Accent the beats! John Lennon, though not a concert pianist, had a creative, intuitive, and forceful approach to the piano. The melody is sweet and pretty here, but the beat never loses its strength, so don't be afraid to add a little power to the piano right now.

Jack and Diane (page 91)

In a newspaper interview back in 2008, John Mellencamp commented on the fact that in many pop circles, depending on when you came of age, this song is his most familiar, almost three decades after releasing it: "It gets played more today in the United States than it did when it came out," he said. "As much as I am a little weary of those two, I don't know any other two people in rock and roll that are more popular than Jack and Diane. Some people probably think there's a place in hell for me because of those two people! But it gave me the keys to do what I want. I've lived the way I wanted to live, sometimes recklessly and stupidly, but still been able to do that. I've been able to live on my whims, that's what Jack and Diane gave me, so I can't hate them too much." A lesson for all you budding songwriters . . . write about characters in the heartland "suckin' on chili dogs" at the "Tastee Freeze" and you, too, might be able to go your own way.

Anyway, Mellencamp brought in a guy named Mick Ronson for his album, *American Fool.* Ronson had made a living and a stellar reputation for himself playing guitar alongside David Bowie in the Spiders from Mars, Bowie's band. After leaving that band, the British guitar superhero signed on to play with Mellencamp, and came up with the signature guitar sound on "Jack and Diane."

Rock steady on this little ditty! The signature *bass riff* (the three eighth notes) needs to be right on time, so be sure to count those measures. The time signature is *cut time* (2/2), so that little riff comes right after the second beat. Then the beat rolls on, just like a couple of restless teens.

X marks the spot where the melody goes missing. On the line "Two American kids. . . " the lyric is spoken, so there is no written piano part. You may choose to play the (x-marked) rhythm and notes from the vocal staff up above. This substitution isn't perfect, but if you're at a party and no singer leaps up, it prevents an awkward pause.

The key here is A major, a common rock key, but Mellencamp gives character to it by mixing up the bass (lower) notes. Using alternate bass notes, for example, an E chord with an (unexpected) A bass note, he reinvents the wheel. Employing this technique throughout, he creates an exceptional tune with just a few common household chords!

Leader of the Band (page 104)

"Leader of the Band" was written for Dan Fogelberg's father, Lawrence "Larry" Fogelberg, a musician, educator, and bandleader. The elder Fogelberg conducted high school bands most of his life and, at the same time, directed the Bradley University band for athletic events and concerts. If you listen to Dan's original, you'll hear his father's arrangement of Sousa's "The Washington Post March" recorded by the UCLA Band. Dan even showed up during the band's recording session to play cymbals. This didn't surprise his dad. "He knows the Sousa accents," Larry said. This isn't to say that his father had the only musical influence on his son. Fogelberg's mother, Margaret, was a music instructor at a high school in Peoria before she met Larry and left work to start a family.

"My father truly gave me more than I could ever repay," said Dan, in an interview after writing the hit. "I was so gratified that I was able to give him that song before he passed on. In his final years he was interviewed many times by the national press because of it. He went out in a blaze of glory, which meant a lot to me and my family."

This band marches to a feeling of two beats per measure. Although the time signature is 4/4, each measure contains two accented beats. So tap your foot (or nod your head) twice per measure to get the rhythm and feel of this acoustic standard.

Be ready for a few flatted notes. This key (A♭) contains four flats: B♭, E♭, A♭, and D♭. Take a few minutes to play some sections focusing only on the flatted notes. After the flatted notes are cemented in your mind, bring the rest of the band in.

The melody leads this band with its flowing turns. Lively and ornate, lots of quarter notes and eighth notes twist down a lyrical river. So, play the right-hand part alone once to get the phrasing and voicings, and then let the melody guide the tune as a good bandleader should!

Leaving on a Jet Plane (page 112)

It seems as if this song has been in the American pop standard songbook forever. But, the fact is, it almost didn't even make the charts. The tune was written by John Denver back in 1967. At the time, he was a member of the Chad Mitchell Trio, and had been suffering from a profound bout of loneliness.

That year, the Chad Mitchell Trio recorded and released Denver's song, and so did another pop group of the time, Spanky & Our Gang. A third act, Peter, Paul and Mary, also covered it on their *Album 1700.* But the breezy, melancholy acoustic croon went nowhere at the time. Then, nearly two years later, Peter, Paul and Mary, a folk-oriented vocal trio with a number of hits already, released the song again, this time as a single. In October of 1969, the trio's own revision of Denver's song hit the charts, where it stayed for 17 weeks, peaking at #1.

Around the same time, Denver released his rendition of the song, on his solo debut, *Rhymes and Reasons.* Rethinking this song in relation to Denver's untimely death in the seat of his own airplane can be a bit melancholy. He died while flying a single engine plane; not on a jet plane of course, but in flight nonetheless.

Hold this favorite on standby until the *chorus.* Be patient while sailing through peaks and valleys as this melody builds and finally soars at the chorus: "Leavin' on a jet plane." Then quickly return to that mellow place and begin to build again.

Highlight the personal touches that make this trip special. In the fifth measure, voice the C note high in the melody over the G chord to create a feeling of longing. Likewise, accent the low D note in measure four. Feel the uneasiness when it's mixed with the C chord above. These wonderful contrasts repeat throughout, providing a melancholy beauty to this masterful ode.

Me and Bobby McGee (page 134)

This is one of those tunes more commonly known not by its composer, but by someone who made the song famous. Kris Kristofferson wrote "Me and Bobby McGee" back in 1968, a short time after he moved to Nashville following a tour of duty in the U.S. Army. The song, co-written by Fred Foster, was picked up and covered by Roger "King of the Road" Miller, but failed to dent the chart. Kristofferson put it on his own debut album, *Kristofferson,* but that too went nowhere, until his label, Monument Records, re-released the album with a new title, *Me and Bobby McGee.* This time it became a moderate success.

In 1969, Kristofferson began dating Janis Joplin, the powerhouse rock and blues singer out of Texas who had been making waves in the post-folk '60s. She decided to cover Kristofferson's tune and did so with such inimitable energy that the tune has since become her own. Sadly, she never enjoyed the success of that tune, which hit #1 in early 1970. Joplin died the previous October and the song was released just weeks later on the posthumous album, *Pearl.*

This road warrior's lament takes it to the next level, literally! Just before the lyric "From the Kentucky coal mines," the key hops aboard the train, one full step up, from G to A. When the three sharps (F♯, C♯, G♯) replace the one (F♯) in the key signature, you know you've arrived!

A classic country blues riff moseys in right before the key change from G to A. Jam a couple times on this sweet little motif and your mind will be halfway to Nashville.

More Than Words (page 146)

Extreme's founding members, Gary Cherone and Nuno Bettencourt started out their professional rock lives as big-time noisemakers. In their hometown of Boston back in 1986 and 1987, they were two-time winners of the top "Metal/Hard Rock Act" prize at the Boston Music Awards. Bettencourt and Cherone routinely wrote blistering, metal-tinged rock characterized by Bettencourt's sizzling shred guitar and Cherone's imposing vocals. Their debut did well enough to warrant a follow-up album and in 1990, they released *Extreme II: Pornograffiti.*

That album featured the acoustic ballad "More Than Words." The tender, exquisitely performed love song, a slow dance/prom night staple, soared to #1 in the spring of 1991 and made Extreme a household name.

However, both Bettencourt and Cherone have blamed Extreme's downturn on the song. The cold hard truth is that this song may have pulled in greater numbers of pop music fans, but its success also gave Extreme the reputation of being a light rock act, with feathery vocals and pretty acoustic guitars. The misconception sent their serious fans elsewhere and sent the band down the path of playing the kind of music they didn't enjoy.

Get into the groove by heating up the beat. Count the 4/4 time signature with a feeling of eight for more precision. Count it this way, however: *one and two and three and four and.* The *one and* method labels the *offbeats,* an important part of any groove!

At the core, this smooth serenade relies on its groove and vibe and really is "more than words." The easy, yet passionate blend of music and words create the "more."

Night Moves (page 152)

Robert Clark Seger first tried his hand at playing music way back in 1961. In interviews, he's credited Elvis and Little Richard for inspiring him to pick up the guitar and start writing songs. Seger was a member of a handful of Detroit bands through the '60s and early '70s, until he formed the Silver Bullet Band in 1974. Always a big hit in his hometown, Seger began picking up fans across the region and even nationally with albums like *Beautiful Loser* and *Live Bullet.* But the real silver bullet came with the release of Seger's 1976 album, *Night Moves.*

Along with the title track, Seger hit his songwriting stride on a handful of memorable tunes like "Mainstreet" and "Rock and Roll Never Forgets." All of Seger's best tracks boast the powerful lure of nostalgia, of wistfully wishing for, or reminiscing about, the good times of the past, the good old days. That lure proved to be Seger's signature, along with his passionate raspy singing voice, both of which sent *Night Moves* into the Top 10 on the album chart, selling over six million copies.

Like a couple of teenage kids sneaking out together, this mid-tempo rock ballad immediately breaks the rules. The *key signature* (indicating the key of G) has one sharp: F♯. However, the first two pages contain only F♮. The F♯ gets its due because F♯ abounds in the chorus, demonstrating why G is the key. Just be ready for those F naturals and you'll have all the right moves!

Pump up the bass. The *bass line* (which consists of the low notes) in this song is played a bit more heavily than in some lighter folk songs. The right hand part takes it easy, simulating a pleasant guitar strum to keep the singer in tune, but the bass line drives this hit.

Don't take the section marked *Freely* too literally. This notation mainly refers to the pauses after each melody line. Don't take too many liberties, because the rhythm, lyric, and melody are written out clearly! Do express yourself but keep it in check or you could be asked to move out of the band.

Nights in White Satin (page 161)

Everyone's favorite Moody Blues song, "Nights in White Satin" wraps up an album called *Days of Future Passed,* a concept album with songs addressing all different times of day. The recording begins with "The Day Begins" and "Dawn Is a Feeling," moves on through "Tuesday Afternoon," and winds it all up with our tune, "Nights." This recording is ambitious, and heralded a change in sound for the band, which began as a bluesy act and then moved into a kind of orchestral psychedelia. Folks in the UK ate it up, but the U.S. kind of scratched its collective head, wondering what to make of all the velvet waistcoats and ruffled shirts. Another problem: "Nights" is over six minutes long. In 1967, the year of its release, that was unheard of. So five years later, after epic songs like "Layla" and "Hey Jude" introduced audiences to lengthier tunes, the Moody Blues reissued the single and this time it stuck. Today, it's one of the best-known tunes of the rock era.

Justin Hayward, who wrote this song at age 19, sold the song rights to skiffle legend Lonnie Donegan, meaning Hayward earned virtually no money from his masterpiece.

Make this night last by keeping it slow. Although the time signature changes from 2/4 to 6/8 early on, the value of the notes remains the same. Roughly, this means the tempo remains slow, from the introduction into the verse.

The melody and lyrics work best when the 6/8 measures are counted as: *one* two three *four* five six . . . with the accents on one and four. This slow standard beat works best to keep the tune smooth as satin.

Fills are little phrases (small groups of notes) between the lyrics. In "Nights in White Satin" the fills function like a *call and response,* the fill imitating and reinforcing the melody. Make the fills a little softer than the melody but a little louder (and brighter) than the rest of the accompaniment and the night will be full indeed.

Norwegian Wood (This Bird Has Flown) (page 164)

Like so many Beatles tunes, this one has been subjected to many interpretations. John Lennon, the principal writer here, said he wanted to pen a song about having an affair, which he indeed was having at the time. Here's a quote from John: "I'd always had some kind of affair going on, so I was trying to be sophisticated in writing about an affair, but in such a smoke-screen way that you couldn't tell." "Norwegian Wood" literally refers to the fake wood used in the manufacture of cheap furniture in the '60s, hence the "falseness," or the backhanded way of saying that something, a relationship for example, is fake.

This is also the first time a pop song featured a sitar, the instrument George Harrison picked up on his pilgrimage to India. Lennon wrote the sitar part into the song before George actually learned how to play the instrument, so there was some reluctance on George's part to try his hand before he was ready to go on record. It helped that John played the sitar line on his guitar, so George could mimic it, which he did, and pretty well at that!

This key (E major) is rock-solid and especially popular with guitar players, so you may run into it often. Find the four sharps: F♯, C♯, G♯, and D♯. If you happen to enjoy playing rock and blues, then knowing this key will serve you well.

A left-handed complement is okay if you're dazzling listeners with these catchy bass patterns. The repeating bass lines here captivate the listener. They capture the songwriter's sentiment: feeling mesmerized by the lovely and mysterious bird. (It may interest you to know that "bird" is British slang for girl.) A smooth bass line seals the deal and sets the mood for this lovely tweet.

The 12/8 time signature may look daunting at first but don't fly away yet. Simply count it as four sets of three: *one two three, one two three, one two three, one two three.* Put a slight accent on each "one" and you've got a dozen reasons to smile!

Please Come to Boston (page 166)

Some refer to Nashville singer and songwriter Dave Loggins as a one-hit wonder, and on the surface that may seem true. "Please Come to Boston," a Top 10 hit in 1974, is a memorable tune, covered by many, including Kenny Chesney, Reba McEntire, and Joan Baez. But behind that one hit is an entire career that measures up to the work of other major songwriters.

He wrote six #1 songs, including Kenny Rogers' "Morning Desire," "Pieces of April" (Three Dog Night), and "Nobody Loves Me Like You Do," a chart-topping duet with Anne Murray that also won him a GRAMMY and a Country Music Association award for Best Vocal Duo in 1985. His accomplishments earned him a place in the 1995 class of the Nashville Songwriters Hall of Fame.

So when you hear "Please Come to Boston," with its melancholy, pleading chorus, and you wonder again who sang this song, don't fall into the trap of thinking it was some one-hit wonder. The man's name is Dave Loggins, no relation to Kenny, and he's written quite a bit more than a single hit song.

Channel easy guitar fingerpicking style to get the right feeling at the piano. Smooth hands link the notes, sustain but don't blur, and give just the right effect for this mellow tale of rambling. If it gets choppy, let your ear guide you back home.

Don't get stuck in a rut, but find and accent the variety. Although the key (B♭) and the tempo (4/4) stay the same throughout, wonderfully nuanced choruses and a bridge provide change. The lyric, "I said ramblin' boy," signals the wonderfully enticing chorus. Likewise the plaintive bridge begins with, "Now the drifter's world," and heralds a different tone. Highlighting those differences proves that variety is the spice of life.

Ribbon in the Sky (page 172)

This ballad first appeared on *Original Musiquarium,* Stevie Wonder's 1982 greatest hits collection. Although some artists do release new songs on hits collections, they don't often end up being hits themselves. Of the four new songs Wonder included on *Original Musiquarium,* only "Ribbon in the Sky" made it into the Top Ten on the R&B chart in 1984 and earned a GRAMMY nomination for Best Male R&B Vocal that year as well. It now lives beside Wonder classics like "You Are the Sunshine of My Life" and "Superwoman" as one of his very best love songs.

Wonder actually wrote this song way back in 1969, over ten years before it came out. Why it took so long to release is anybody's guess. But this song soon began living in the shadows of "Ebony and Ivory," Wonder's duet with Paul McCartney. Released just after "Ribbon in the Sky," "Ebony and Ivory" dominated charts across the globe, while at the same time being derided as super-sweet and not deserving of a place in either of the artists' canons.

Stevie Wonder brings songs in uncommon keys to life. Here he tosses the key of D♭ into the ring. With five rich flats: B♭, E♭, A♭, D♭, and G♭, this key (and tune) shines like a new Steinway. As the direction indicates, play this celestial beauty *slowly, with expression.*

The sky is the limit for Stevie Wonder. The key changes from D♭ to D, with two sharps (F♯ and C♯) for a brief period. Worry not, a third key quickly takes over and finishes up the piece. The final key of E♭ (with B♭, E♭, and A♭) ties up the package and takes this wonderful journey home!

Get into the groove, based on an accented third beat. In 4/4, giving the third beat an accent adds a rocking motion, countering the strong first beat. The second and fourth beats stay in the background, letting the first and third beat battle for your feet.

Sailing (page 178)

Christopher Cross had a voice made for radio and for a four-year stint between 1980 and 1983, radio loved Mr. Cross. There was a creamy sweetness to the way he sang, and a soft-rock romanticism that he captured on his best songs.

"Sailing" won GRAMMYs for "Record of the Year" and "Song of the Year" in 1980 and pretty much dominated the charts for the entire summer of 1980. Many of us took up sailing that summer largely because Cross made it sound like it was the perfect outing for a date, and an easy way to find privacy.

The following year Cross won an Oscar with songwriting legends Burt Bacharach and Carole Bayer Sager, this time for Best Song with "Arthur's Theme (The Best That You Can Do)" from the Dudley Moore movie *Arthur.* His second album, *Another Page,* released in 1983, featured "Think of Laura," his last Top 40 hit. At the time, musical tastes were changing quickly and Cross's smooth croon fell out of favor.

Sweet sound waves rise and fall to a gentle 2/2 beat. Also called *cut time,* two strong beats contrast the rolling patterns based on the calm, steady key of A major.

Don't jazz up this tune, which takes its cue from classical music. The lower (bass) notes move independently from the upper notes, very common in classical forms. Also, take a look at how the notes move in half-steps (for example: G♯ to A and D to C♯). This *chromatic* motion gives the song a smooth, majestic feel, as if gliding over a timeless ocean.

Suite: Judy Blue Eyes (page 185)

The title of this song, an ode to Judy Collins, plays on the word "sweet." In fact, the song is a series of musical compositions all in the same key, making it quite literally a "suite." Back in the late '60s, Stills had dated, and subsequently lost, Collins, and wrote this song to win her back. Stills and Collins had an intense and turbulent relationship.

In the first song of the suite, Stills recalls happier times the couple shared, while at the same time realizing their relationship had changed. In the second song, he pleads with her for one more chance, with the simple question, "What have you got to lose?" In the third song, Stills recalls how happy he was with her and asks what he can do to win her back. As the song fades, he lapses into a little Spanish, a language he picked up in Costa Rica, where he attended school briefly.

Stills wrote a handful of other notable songs dedicated to Collins, including "Bluebird," "You Don't Have to Cry," and "Bluebird Revisited." In a 1971 interview, a *Rolling Stone* reporter asked him why so many of his songs were about Collins. Stills answered, "Well, there are three things men can do with women: love them, suffer for them, or turn them into literature. I've had my share of success and failure at all three."

Recreate voices with a choir of keys. The melody mixes a single vocal line with a mix of three-part harmonies. Play this contrast to grand effect. Also balance jaunty rhythms with held notes. Use your imagination to let your fingers do the singing.

Let the funk shine in the bass line. Run through the tune playing only the left hand bass (lower notes). Notice how rich and lively the bass is for a tune often associated with straightforward folk music.

Keep this suite sweet by catching the change of key near the end of the song. The key of E major does a quick change to A major. These are similar keys, so just drop the D♯ from E major and you're home.

Summer Breeze (page 198)

Jim Seals and Dash Crofts released their first album as a twosome in 1969, but they didn't get their first hit until three years later, when "Summer Breeze" played the airwaves in the summer of 1972. The boys followed that up with a small bunch of memorable tunes, including "Diamond Girl," "Get Closer," "I'll Play for You," and "We May Never Pass This Way Again," all Top 40 hits.

And here's another factoid. Jim's brother Dan was "Dan" in England Dan and John Ford Coley, themselves masters of acoustic pop ("I'd Really Love to See You Tonight" and "Love Is the Answer" among their hits) in the late '70s.

Be ready for an E major chord in measure seven, following a breezy E minor introduction. "Summer Breeze" is in the key of E minor (note the lone F# in the key signature). The minor to major shift highlights the opening lyric. Prepare for other neat changes to waft through your mind in this mellow classic.

Don't repeat and fade away. *Repeat and fade,* the marked ending to this tune, can be tricky to pull off on piano (though easy for radio DJs who have a song to fade into). To remedy that, find some good notes with which to end the fade. Try the first notes of the last measure (they are marked as an Em7 chord). As you soften, you'll have a fade and an ending, too.

The key here is E minor. If you think it's G major, don't worry. Your mind is not full of jasmine. You are at least half right! E minor is the *relative minor* key to G major, with the same key signature (one F♯). The two keys are related, but on good terms, so songwriters shift from one to the other, because it sounds good and keeps you on your toes.

Take Me Home, Country Roads (page 204)

Denver never lived in West Virginia. In fact, when this song came out, he had never even *been* there. Denver moved from his birthplace in New Mexico to Los Angeles in 1964, where he started his career with the Chad Mitchell Trio. So, what's the deal with West Virginia?

Denver worked with Bill Danoff and Taffy Nivert extensively, and this song was their most successful collaboration. It peaked at #2 in 1971 and helped Denver earn superstar status. Danoff and Nivert, working together as "Fat City," sang backing vocals on the recording. But that's not their only claim to fame. In 1976, Bill and Taffy, along with John Carroll and his future wife Margot Chapman, had a hit with Starland Vocal Band called "Afternoon Delight." Remember that one? SVB recorded for John Denver's own Windsong label.

Other collaborations between Danoff and Denver include "I Guess He'd Rather Be in Colorado" and "Baby, You Look Good to Me Tonight."

Start this journey off right by solving the mystery of the B♯ note in measures 2 and 4. B♯ may catch you off-guard, because technically, B♯ is also the C note on the piano.

Take a quick pit stop when you reach "I hear her voice" and ease the bright country tempo a bit. Don't barrel through this subtle change in tone because a thoughtful, more personal lyric is also in tow. Then ride the bright new chord progression (F♯m to G at "drivin' down the road") back to the chorus that takes you home!

Teach Your Children (page 209)

Graham Nash wrote this song as a member of his original hit-making band The Hollies ("Look Through Any Window," "Bus Stop," "Carrie Anne"). The Hollies were immensely popular in Britain in the mid-1960s, finishing only behind The Shadows and The Beatles in number of hit songs.

Nash left the band in 1968, feeling hemmed in by The Hollies' reputation as teen stars. He had long sought to write more personal, less pop-oriented material and leaving was the only way he could accomplish that. "Teach Your Children" is the kind of song Nash yearned to write: serious, political, meaningful, and enduring. He tied in with Stephen Stills and David Crosby on a 1968 trip to Laurel Canyon, a burg outside of Los Angeles famous for its songwriters and recreational drug use.

His later work with these songwriters helped him define an era for the Woodstock generation, and his canon with Crosby, Stills, Nash and Young earned Nash a berth in the Rock and Roll Hall of Fame. The former Manchester lad will be inducted a second time in 2010 — a rarity only afforded pop's most select talent — as a founding member of The Hollies.

School your fingers well to master the grace notes found in measures two, four, and five. *Grace notes* are small, with a line through the stem, appearing just before regular notes. Play them quickly yet smoothly and don't forget the jump from E to F♯ in measures two and five.

Slow and steady makes the grade here, rhythmic but not bouncy. A smooth attack allows wonderful harmonies to blend together. Glide from one to the next, leaving leapfrog for later in the schoolyard.

Tears in Heaven (page 216)

When unspeakable tragedy befell Eric Clapton in 1991 — the death of his young son — he did what any musician would do: He wrote a song about it. At the time, Clapton was working with Will Jennings on a movie soundtrack to the film *Rush.* Clapton had just finished writing a song for the end credits of the movie, called "Help Me Up," when he identified a spot in the film for another track. He had the first verse of "Tears in Heaven" written already, but found it too painful to finish, so he handed over the unfinished track to Jennings for completion. Jennings blanched at the request; the song was just too personal, he felt, for anybody other than Clapton to write. But he eventually acquiesced and carried the song through its final verses, including the couplet about time: "Time can bring you down . . . Time can bend your knees." Jennings had some pretty impressive credentials, including "Looks Like We Made It," "Up Where We Belong," and "Higher Love," and Clapton entrusted him with this weighty entry as well.

This heavenly ballad uses earthy bottom tones (the bass line) to chart its path. Try the first few lower note patterns, solo, with an expressive left hand. The line functions like a sweet melody, replete with easy step-wise motion, so voice it like a low melody yearning to ascend.

Prepare twice here: Once for three sharps in the key of A Major (F♯, C♯, and G♯), and then for variations on the key. The verse stays tightly in A major, but the chorus ("I must be strong") and the bridge ("Time can bring you down") take wonderful excursions. Well placed sharps, flats, and naturals bring emotion to this poignant masterpiece.

Note the classic gospel riff (A/E to E) at the line "saw you in heaven." Billy Preston employed this standard technique in The Beatles' classic "Don't Let Me Down." Eric Clapton is well known for carrying on traditions of early blues and gospel music. He also promotes recognition of often forgotten black artists who planted the seeds of rock and roll.

Time in a Bottle (page 226)

Funny how things work out . . . Jim Croce wrote this acoustic classic for his first album, *You Don't Mess Around with Jim,* released in 1972. But two singles off that album, "Operator (That's Not the Way It Feels)" and the title track, both did really well. So when it was time for single number three, Croce had another album done and ready for release. That album, *Life and Times,* had another memorable tune ready to roll for its first single, "Bad, Bad Leroy Brown."

Eventually "Time in a Bottle" resurfaced when it appeared on the soundtrack to a made-for-TV movie starring Desi Arnaz Jr., about a woman dying of cancer. Not that Croce's melancholy tune was about mortality so much. He wrote it for his infant son Adrian, who later followed in his dad's footsteps as a songwriter.

A couple of weeks after this song came out as a single, Croce died in a plane crash that killed all six people aboard. The song went posthumously to #1. Two other deceased artists had their songs go to #1 in the rock era, Janis Joplin ("Me and Bobby McGee") and Otis Redding ("[Sittin' On] The Dock of the Bay").

Bottle up the energy and keep this one slow! In 3/4 time this ballad's tempo and mellow tone will have you swaying more than waltzing. Keep the tempo in check and relish the melody, plus sweet climbs and descents between lyrics. The correct timing makes this fine wine age just right.

Know the key but be ready for changes. A key change comes at the lyric, "never seems to be enough time." At the chorus, D minor (with one flat: B♭) becomes D major (with two sharps: C♯ and F♯). The change is temporary, however, and D minor resumes at the coda. Let the chorus pour out bittersweet nectar of love remembered.

Turn! Turn! Turn! (To Everything There Is a Season) (page 230)

Some songs are hefty enough to have a life of their own, and this is one of them. Sometime in the 1950s, folk icon Pete Seeger lifted the lyrics of this song almost verbatim from the Bible's Book of Ecclesiastes. He slapped a folky refrain on it, "Turn, turn, turn," which he later likened to "twinkle, twinkle little star," and began performing it around the Greenwich Village area during the early stages of the folk boom. The Limeliters, another folk act in New York City at the time, liked the song enough to record it in early 1962, before Seeger himself did later that same year. The guitarist for the Limeliters was none other than Jim "Roger" McGuinn, soon to be the guitarist for the Byrds, who'd go on to give this song immortality.

The Byrds mined the folk music world for their first single, Bob Dylan's "Mr. Tambourine Man," and hit the jackpot with it. After stumbling briefly with another Dylan tune for a follow-up, they found Seeger's tune for their third single and the rest, as is so often said, is history.

The rhythm of this beautiful scripture set to music isn't as simple as it looks. The lyric "turn," always repeated three times against a 2/2 (cut time) beat, produces unexpected (and unorthodox) rhythms and accents. Notice how "turn" in measure seven (a quarter note) is shorter than the other two "turns" preceding it. In measures nine and ten the three "turns" have the same time value (half notes). Be vigilant to these quirks and you will hear what makes this sublime hymn so sublime.

The volume *(dynamics)* is louder on the verse ("A time to . . . ") than on the chorus ("To everything . . . "). Don't shout it from the mountain, though, because the *p* (piano) marking in the first measure indicates soft in Italian. Then find *mf* (mezzo forte), moderately loud, in measure fourteen. Continue these volume changes throughout, keeping the tempo and key firmly in place.

Vincent (Starry Starry Night) (page 221)

When Don McLean released his second album, *American Pie,* the song became a hit, and since its release has been spun three or four million times. McLean has always tried to distance himself from that tune, choosing to let his entire oeuvre speak for itself. His *second* most popular composition, spun maybe two million times since its release, is "Vincent (Starry Starry Night)."

The song, an elegy to Vincent Van Gogh, is a touching tribute to the artist who struggled with sanity and drug addictions. Few have succeeded as well as McLean in singing so beautifully about such a tortured soul.

McLean wrote the song, also known as "Starry, Starry Night," in the fall of 1970 while he was teaching and living in Stockbridge, Massachusetts. McLean wrote "Vincent" in his apartment, which was full of antiques. The inspiration came to him one morning while he was sitting on the veranda looking at a book about Vincent Van Gogh. He came across a print of Van Gogh's painting, "Starry Night," and realized there was a song in the painting.

Left-hand patterns should be as steady as the hand of a clock ticking. Stretch the fingers wide to keep high and low notes smooth. Avoid using a right hand dip to help with the low notes. Like carefully mixed colors on a painter's palette, a smooth, slow *tempo* will mesmerize your listeners.

Keep those stars shining as new chords shoot across the musical sky after the second ending. Chords not usually associated with this key, G Major, appear at the words, "and when no hope was left." A flurry of sharps and flats paint the picture. The key signature stays the same, so maintain the F♯. Play this stunning swirl of chords and hear the melancholy joy this canvas exudes!

Wanted Dead or Alive (page 234)

This big, power metal ballad became a signature of Jon Bon Jovi and guitarist Richie Sambora, who provided the recognizable acoustic hook opening the song. It also encapsulated Bon Jovi's infatuation with cowboys and the Old West by comparing life on the road as a rock and roll band in a "steel horse" (tour bus) with a six-string (close to six-shooter), to a solitary outlaw gallivanting around the prairie. This romantic ideal later came to fruition on "Blaze of Glory," another western-tinged rock hymn.

Some say this tune, with its lush acoustic sound, launched the "unplugged" concept on music television. In 1989, Sambora and Bon Jovi played this song at the MTV Video Music Awards as a duet on acoustic guitars. The song was originally featured on the band's immensely successful album, *Slippery When Wet.* It became the album's third single, and the third one to hit the Top 10, right behind "You Give Love a Bad Name" and "Livin' on a Prayer."

Be on the lookout for *accidentals!* Accidentals are sharps or flats written next to individual notes. The key signature indicates C Major (no sharps or flats). But this key, like the Wild West, is unpredictable, so stage a search for accidentals throughout. Remember, once a note has been marked with a sharp (♯) or flat (♭) sign, it remains altered throughout that measure.

Be a performer. Take the introduction slowly and milk it a bit. The signature riff that opens the tune is well known and folks enjoy grooving on it, so don't rush — relish its appeal. When the riff appears later in the song, do likewise. That said, rock the melody with a straight-ahead tempo once the song has begun and keep the speed up for the bulk of it. Then let the performer in you sense when it's time to stop, and start up the rodeo!

Yesterday (page 246)

"Yesterday" is the #1 pop song of all time, according to *Rolling Stone* and MTV. It has also been covered by more artists than any other song in history, around 3,000.

Paul McCartney wrote this tune in 1964, but it ended up missing two album cycles — *Beatles for Sale* and *A Hard Day's Night* — before finally ending up on *Help!* In fact, the song was around so long, and McCartney had talked about it so much, that the other Beatles were sick of hearing about it. For most of that time, Paul admitted he didn't have any lyrics to go along with the piano melody. He jokingly referred to it as "Scrambled Eggs," which seems like a flippant moniker for what would later become pop music's best-loved song.

Depending on whom you believe, it was either written in a dream, or while on tour in France. It lives as the first time The Beatles relied on the performance of a single member for any of its songs. Though it has its fans, to say the least, one of them is not Bob Dylan, who considered "Yesterday" very average. "You can find millions of better songs in the Library of Congress," he quipped.

Recall the slower pace of the "good ol' days" as you begin what is perhaps the ultimate ballad of love lost. Melt into the moment when you find the correct pace. A slow speed allows you to savor classic passages like the bass riff following "She wouldn't say." Play, and live, steady and slow and you'll have no regrets, today or tomorrow.

Repeat the introductory measures if it feels right. Those simple opening bars are familiar to listeners and also set the tone. At a gathering, folks may want to hear the beginning for an extra moment. The two opening measures are identical, so repeating a measure or two there won't hurt anyone. But don't dawdle, or they'll think you've forgotten the tune!

Be ready for rich and beautiful chord changes, including a few extra sharps and flats. As songwriters, The Beatles were not afraid to show off their range. Accidentals like B♮ and a C♯ appear throughout. Don't forget B♭ in the key signature, either, because F Major is the key of this timeless classic!

You've Got a Friend (page 240)

Carole King wrote this song and included it on her landmark album *Tapestry* in 1971. But it was popularized, of course, by "Sweet Baby James," also known as James Taylor, later that same year. Interestingly, another artist, Dusty Springfield, recorded a version of the song in 1971, while doing her own landmark album, *Dusty in Memphis.* But because Springfield's album featured R&B, recorded in Memphis with a soul act called the Memphis Cats, the King tune didn't exactly fit the mood. (It was later released on the deluxe version of *In Memphis.*)

This song, incredibly, stands as Taylor's only #1 hit. It topped the charts in June of 1971, won Taylor a GRAMMY for Best Male Vocal Performance, and won King a GRAMMY for Song of the Year. On the strength of the song, Taylor's album, *Mud Slide Slim,* climbed all the way to #2 on the *Billboard* chart. But, in one of pop music's little ironies, the recording fell short of the top slot by one, which happened to be occupied already by Carole King's own *Tapestry.*

The right key opens this friendly door. Get familiar with A Major's three sharps (F♯, C♯, and G♯) and embark on an exquisite journey into jazz. Carole King, a songwriter's songwriter, remains no stranger to textured, interesting chords. With the A Major key set in your mind, adapt quickly to its many variations. For example, two altered tones (D♯ and E♯) appear early on, in the fourth measure. ***Note:*** E♯ is another name for F♮, so E♯ and F are, in fact, the same note!

Extended major chords ring out, especially in the chorus at the lyric, "You just call out my name." At those lyrics, the musical underpinnings feature an Amaj9 chord and a Dmaj7 chord, respectively. Be sure you play G♯ (not the blues 7th note G♮) in the Amaj9 chord. Likewise on Dmaj7, hit C♯ (not C♮) and all your friends will soon find you at the jazz club.

Me and Bobby McGee

Words and Music by Kris Kristofferson and Fred Foster

* Vocal written one octave higher than sung.

pulled my har - poon out of my dirt - y red ban - dan - a. I was
G7
C
play - in' soft while Bob - by sang the blues, yeah.
G
Wind - shield wip - ers slap - pin' time, I's hold - in' Bob - by's hand in mine;
D
D7
C
we sang ev - 'ry song that driv - er knew, yeah.
Free - dom's just an - oth - er word for

G
D7
C/D
D7
noth-in' left to lose.
Noth - in', I mean noth - in', hon', if it ain't
G
C
free, no, no.
Yeah, feel - in' good was eas - y, Lord,
G
D7
when he sang the blues.
You know, feel - in' good was good e - nough for me,
D
G
good e - nough for me an' my Bob - by Mc - Gee.
8va

A
D/E
From the Ken - tuck - y coal mine to the
A
D/E
A
Cal - i - for - nia sun, hey, Bob - by shared the se - crets of my
E7
soul. Through all kinds of weath - er, through
ev - 'ry - thing we done, yeah, Bob - by ba - by kept me from the cold.

A
D/E
A
One day a - near Sa - lin - as, Lord,
I let him slip a - way.
A7
He's look - in' for that home and I hope he
D
finds it.
But I'd trade all of my to - mor - rows for one
A
E
sin - gle yes - ter - day to be hold - in' Bob - by's bod - y next to mine.

D/E
D
Free - dom's just an - oth - er word for
A
E
noth - in' left to lose.
Noth - in', and that's all that Bob - by left
A
D
me, yeah.
But if feel - in' good was eas - y, Lord,
A
E
when he sang the blues,
hey, feel - in' good was good e - nough for me,

E7
mm hmm,
good e - nough for me and my Bob - by Mc -
A
Gee.
La da da da, la da da da, la da da da da da da,
mp
E
la da da da da la da la da Bob-by Mc-Gee, yeah.
La da la la la la,
la da da da da,
la la la la la Bob - by Mc -

A
Gee.
La da da la da da la da da la da da,
la da lo la da da la da la,
hey now, Bob - by, lo now, Bob-by Mc - Gee,
mf
E7
yeah.
Lo na lo na na lo na, na,
lo na na na
na na na na na na na na na na na,
hey now, Bob - by, lo now, Bob-by Mc - Gee,

A
yeah. And then when I called him my lov - er, called him my man; I said I
f
called him my lov - er, did the best I can. Come on, hey now, Bob - by, now, hey now, Bob - by Mc - Gee,
E7
yeah. Lo la lo la lo la lo la lo la lo
la lo la lo lo, ley, hey, hey, Bob - by Mc - Gee,

A
Lord.

E7

A

E7

A

E7
La la la la la la la la la la la

A
la la la la, hey, hey, hey, Bob-by Mc-Gee, ah.

More Than Words

Words and Music by Nuno Bettencourt and Gary Cherone

* Recorded a half step lower.

Am7
C
D
Dsus
Em
want you not to say, but if you on - ly knew
have to do is close your eyes and just reach out your hands
G/B
Am7
D7
G
how eas - y it would be to show
and touch me. Hold me close don't ev -
Bm7/F♯
Em
G/B
Am7
me how you feel. More than words is
- er let me go. More than words is
D7
G7
G7/B
C
Cm
all you have to do to make it real.
all I ev - er need - ed you to show.
Then you would-
3fr

G
Em
G/B
Em11
5fr
G/B
- n't have to say that you love me 'cause
Am7
D7
G
G/B
G
G/B
I'd al - read - y know. What would you do
D/F♯
Em
G/B
Bm7
C
if my heart was torn in two? More than words
Am
D7
G
to show you feel that your love for me is real.

G/B
G
G/B
D/F♯
Em
What would you say if I took
G/B
Bm7
C
Am7
those words a - way? Then you could - n't make things new
To Coda
D7
G
G/B
C
just by say - in' "I love you."
Am7
C
D5
5fr
D7
G
La di da da di da di dai dai da. More than words.

G/B
C(add2)
Am7
La di da da di da.
D7
D.S. al Coda
CODA
D7
G
G/B
C
-in' "I love you."
Am7
C
D5
5fr
D7
G
La di da da di da di dai dai da.
More than words.
C(add2)
Am7
1, 2
C
La di da da di da di dai dai da.

D5
D7
G
3
C
D5
D
More than words.
More than words,
La da dat da da da.
G
D/F♯
Fmaj13
ooh,
rit.
E(add4)
Am7
D
ooh.
(Guitar cadenza)
More than
Slowly
G
Csus2
G/B
Gm/B♭
Am7
G
words.

Night Moves

Words and Music by Bob Seger

C
F
G
and points all her own, sit-tin' way up high,
F
C
F
way up firm and high.
G
F
Out past the corn - fields, where the woods got heav - y,
C
F
G
out in the back seat of my Six - ty Chev - y,
work-in' on mys-t'ries with - out

F
C
D
any clues,
workin' on our
Em
D
C
D
Em
D
night moves,
try'n' to make some
front page, drive-in news.
C
D
Em
D
C
Workin' on our night moves
G
F
C
in the summertime.
Mm,

F
G
F
in the sweet
sum-mer-time.
C
F
G
We were-n't in love. Oh,
F
C
F
no, far from it.
We were-n't search - in for some pie - in-the - sky sum - mit.
G
F
C
We were just young and rest - less and bored,
liv-ing by the sword.

F
G
F
And we'd steal a - way ev - 'ry chance we could,
C
F
to the back room, to the al - ley, or the trust - y woods.
G
F
I used her, she used me, but nei - ther one cared.
C
D
Em
D
We were get - tin' our share, work - in' on our night moves,

C
D
Em
D
C
D
try'n' to lose the awk-ward teen-age blues, work-in' on our
Em
D
C
G
night moves. It was sum-mer-time.
F
C
F
Mm,
G
F
C
sweet sum-mer-time, sum-mer-time.

D
Em
D
G
G7
3fr
Cmaj7
G
And oh, the won-der.
Cmaj7
3
We felt the light-ning. Yeah,
3
F
D
and we wait-ed on the thun - der,
wait-ed on the thun - der.

G
Freely
Cmaj7
I a-woke last night to the sound of thun-der.
How far off, I
G
Cmaj7
sat and won-dered.
Start-ed hum-ming a song from nine-teen six-ty-two.
3
Em
C
Em
Ain't it fun-ny how the night moves
when you just don't seem to
have as much to lose.

C
Em
C
Cmaj7
G
Strange how the night moves, _
with au - tumn clos - ing in. _
Tempo I
G
F
C
F
G
G
F
C
1-7
F
Night moves.
Lead vocal ad lib. to end
Night moves.
8
Em
Bm
Am7
C
G

Nights in White Satin

Words and Music by Justin Hayward

G
F
Em
writ - ten,
nev - er mean - ing to send.
go - ing through,
they can't un - der - stand.
D
Em
Beau - ty I'd al - ways missed
with these eyes be -
Some try to tell me
thoughts they can - not de -
D
C
G
fore.
Just what the truth is
fend,
just what you want to be
F
Em
A
I can't say an - y - more.
'Cause I
love you,
you'll be in the end.
And I

C
yes, I love you.
Oh, how I
1
Em
D
Em
D
love you.
2
Em
D
Em
love you.
Oh, how I love
D
Em
Em7
you.

Norwegian Wood
(This Bird Has Flown)

Words and Music by John Lennon and Paul McCartney

Em
F♯m7
B
I looked a-round and I no-ticed there was-n't a chair.
told her I did-n't and crawled off to sleep in the bath.
E
Bm7
A
E
I sat on a rug, bid-ing my time, drink-ing her wine.
And when I a-woke I was a-lone; this bird had flown.
Bm7
A
E
We talked un-til two and then she said, "It's time for bed."
So I lit a fire, is-n't it good Nor-we-gian wood.
Bm7
A
E
rit.

Please Come to Boston

Words and Music by Dave Loggins

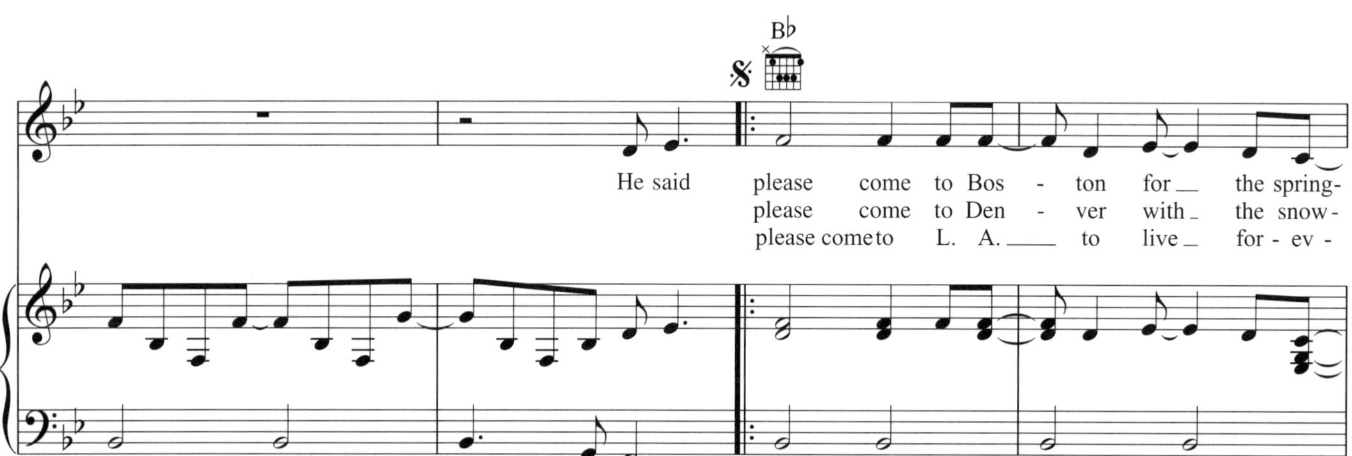

E♭
3fr
and they've got lots of room.
tains so far we can't be found,
a - lone is just too hard to build.
and
I
F
B♭
You can sell your paint - ings on the side - walk
throw "I love you" ech - oes down the can - yons
live in a house that looks out o - ver the o - cean.
Gm
3fr
E♭
3fr
by a ca - fé where I hope to be work - in' soon.
and then lie a - wake at night un - til they come back a - round.
And there's some stars that fell from the sky liv - in' up on the hill.
B♭
Please come to Bos - ton, I said no,
Please come to Den - ver, I just said no,
Please come to L. A., I just said no,

F
B♭
boy, would
boy, won't
boy, won't
you come home to me.
I said
ram - blin' boy, why don't you set - tle down.
Bos - ton ain't your
Den - ver ain't your
L. A. can't be your
kind of town.
There ain't no gold and there ain't no - bod - y like
To Coda
E♭
3fr
Cm7
Fsus
me.
I'm the num - ber one fan of the man from Ten - nes - see.

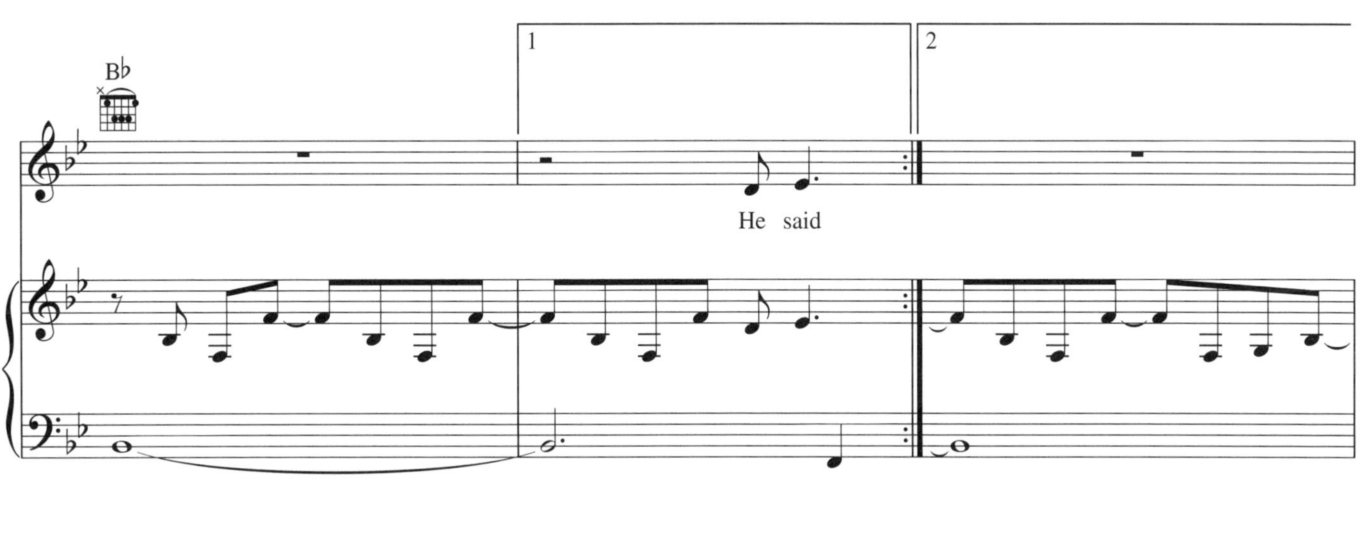
B♭
1
2
He said

E♭
3fr

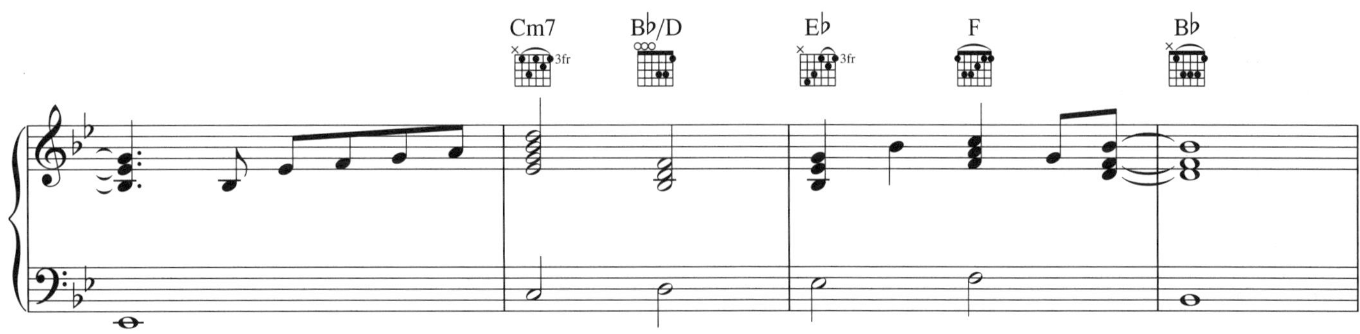
Cm7
3fr
B♭/D
E♭
3fr
F
B♭

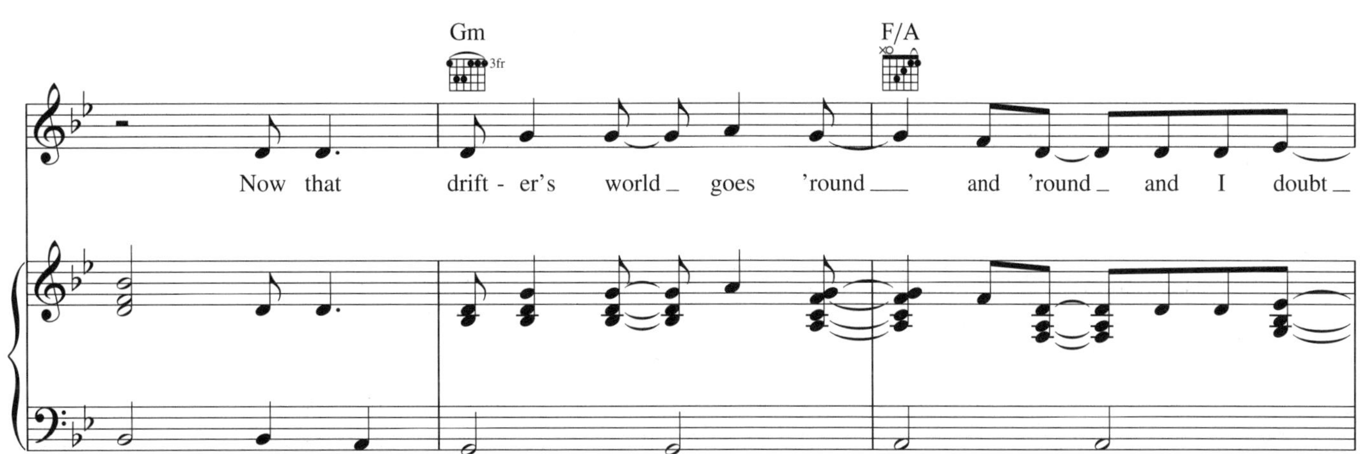
Gm
3fr
F/A
Now that drift - er's world _ goes 'round ___ and 'round _ and I doubt _

Eb
F
Bb
Gm
if it's ev - er gon - na stop. But of all the dreams he's lost
F/A
Eb
or found and all that I ain't got, he still needs to
Cm7
Fsus
F
D.S. al Coda
lean to some - bod - y he can sing to. He said
CODA
Eb
Cm7
no - bod - y like me. I'm the num - ber one fan of the man

Fsus
F
B♭
Cm
B♭/D
3fr
from Ten-nes-see.
I'm the num-ber one fan of the man
E♭
F
E♭(add2)
3fr
6fr
from Ten - nes - see,
Ten-nes - see.
Repeat and Fade
Optional Ending
B♭

Ribbon in the Sky

Words and Music by Stevie Wonder

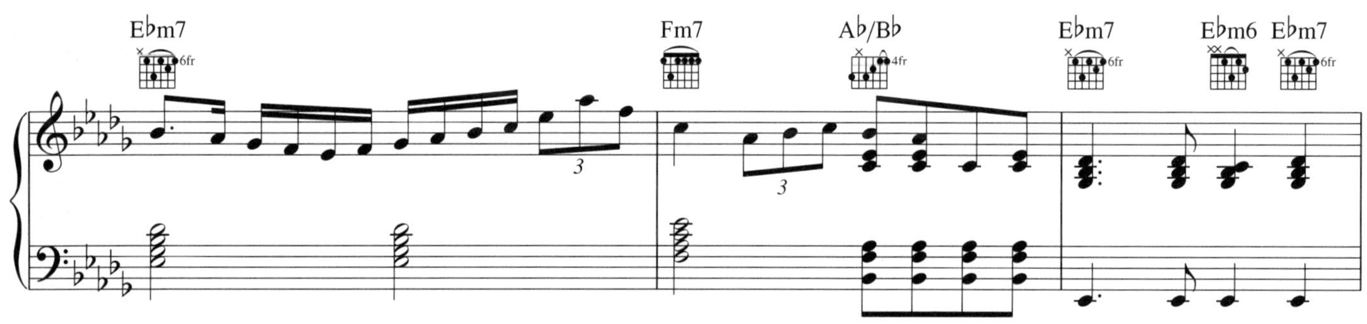

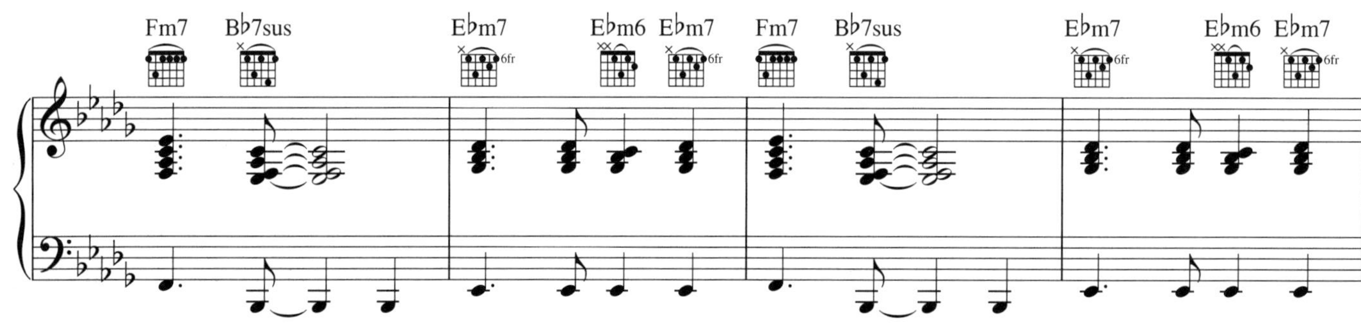

Ebm7
Fm7
Bb7sus
Ebm7
long for this night I prayed that a star would guide
lowed, may I touch your hand, and if pleased may I
Fm7
Bb7sus
Ebm7
Fm7
Bb7sus
you my way to share with me this spe - cial day where a
once a - gain, so that you too will un - der - stand there's a
1
Ebm11
Ebm/F
Ebm/Gb
Eb/G
Gb/Ab
Cbmaj7
Ab7sus
rib - bon's in the sky for our love. If al -
2
Ebm11
Ebm/F
Ebm/Gb
Eb/G
Gb/Ab
Db
Ebm7
Ebm6
rib - bon in the sky for our love. Doo
(Vocal ad lib.)

Fm7
B♭7sus
E♭m7
E♭m6
E♭m7
doo doo
Fm7
B♭7sus
E♭m7
E♭m6
E♭m7
Fm7
B♭7sus
doo doo
doo
E♭m11
E♭m/F
E♭m/G♭
E♭/G
G♭/A♭
C♭/A
A9
doo.
This is
Em7
F♯m7
B7sus
Em7
not a co - in - ci - dence, and far more than a

F♯m7
B7sus
Em7
F♯m7
B7sus
luck - y chance, but what is that was al - ways meant is our
Em11
Em/F♯
Em/G
G/A
A♭/B♭
rib - bon in the sky for our love; love we can't lose,
Fm7
Gm7
C7sus
Fm7
with God on our side. We'll find strength in each
Gm7
C7sus
Fm7
Gm7
C7sus
tear we cry. From now on it will be you and I and our

Fm11
Fm7/G
Fm7/A♭
F/A
A♭/B♭
Gm7♭5
C9
rib - bon in the sky,
rib - bon in the sky, a
Fm7
Fm6
Gm7
C7sus
rib - bon in the sky for our love.
Ooh,
ooh
ooh.
Vocal ad lib.
Doo doo
ooh
doo doo doo.
D♭maj7

Fm7
Fm6
Fm7
Gm7
C7sus
Fm7
Fm6
Fm7
Instrumental ad lib.

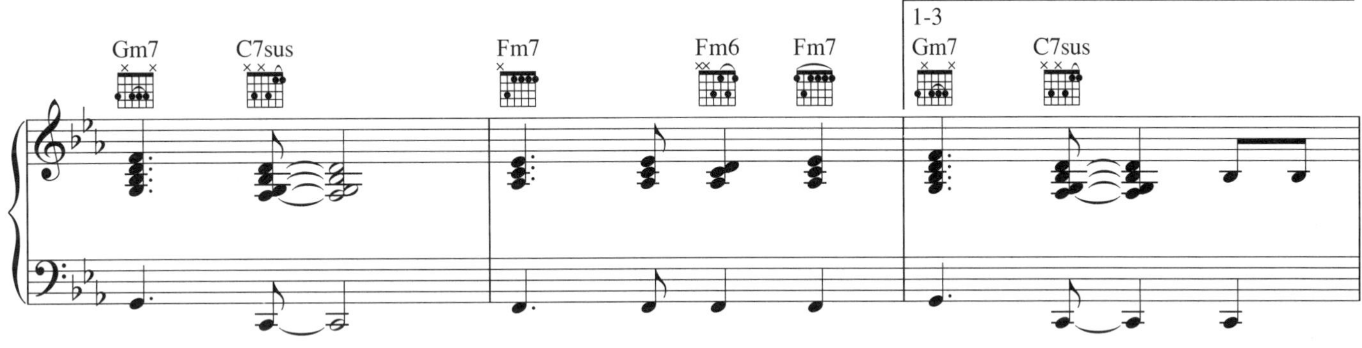
Gm7
C7sus
Fm7
Fm6
Fm7
1-3
Gm7
C7sus

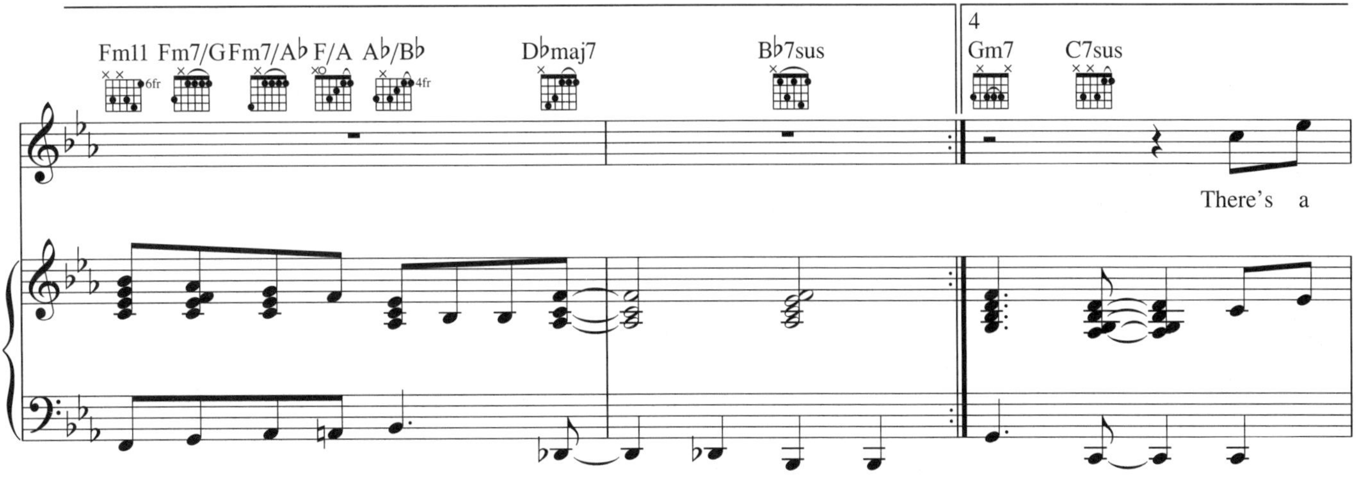
Fm11
Fm7/G
Fm7/A♭
F/A
A♭/B♭
D♭maj7
B♭7sus
4
Gm7
C7sus
There's a

Fm11
Fm/G
Fm/A♭
F/A
A♭/B♭
E♭(add9)
E♭
rib - bon in the sky for our love.
rit.

Sailing

Words and Music by Christopher Cross

E/D
A/D
E/D
A/D
- vas can do mir - a - cles,
just you wait and see.
E/A
A
Believe me.
E/A
A
A/C♯
D(add2)
It's not far to nev - er - nev -
far back to san -
- er land, no rea - son to pre - tend,
i - ty, at least it's not for me,
and if the wind
and if the wind

F♯m9
is right you can find the joy of in - no - cence a - gain.
is right you can sail a - way and find se - ren - i - ty.
E/D
A/D
Oh, the can - vas can do mir - a - cles,
E/D
A/D
E/A
A
just you wait and see. Be - lieve me.
E/A
A

E/A
A
E/A
A
Sail - ing takes me a - way to where
D(add2)
I've al - ways heard it could be.
Bm9
Just a dream and the wind to car -
F♯m9
C♯m7
D(add2)
- ry me, and soon I will be free.

To Coda
E/A
A
E/A
A
Fan - ta - sy, it gets the best of me
F♯m9
when I'm sail - ing.
E/D
A/D
All caught up in the rev -

E/D
A/D
- er - ie,
ev - 'ry word is a sym - pho - ny. Won't you be - lieve
E/A
A
E/A
A
me?
E/A
A
Sail - ing takes me a - way
E/A
A
D(add2)
to where I've al - ways heard it could be.

Just a dream
and the wind to car - ry me, and soon I will be free.
Bm9
F♯m9
C♯m7
D(add2)
A
D.S. al Coda
Well, it's not
CODA
Play 3 times
8vb

Suite: Judy Blue Eyes

Words and Music by Stephen Stills

A7sus
E
D/A
A
Some - times it hurts so bad - ly I
Don't let the past re - mind us of
E
B
E/B
B
E/B
B
A
must cry out loud.
what we are not now.
I am lone - ly.
I am not dream - ing.
E
B
A
I am yours, you are mine, you are what you are.
1
A7sus
E
A
You make it hard. Re -
2
A7sus
You make it

E
hard.
Tear - ing your - self
A
E
B
a - way from me now, you are free
A
E
and I am cry - ing.
This does not

A
E
B
mean I don't love you, I do, that's for - ev - er,
A
yes, and for al - ways.
I am yours,
E
B
A
A7sus
you are mine, you are what you are.
You make it
E
A
E
D/A
hard.
Some - thing in - side is

A
E
E/B
B
tell-ing me that I've got your se - cret.
Are you still
A
A7
E
D/A
lis - t'ning?
Fear is the lock and
A
E
B
laugh - ter the key to your heart,
and I
A
E
B
love you.
I am yours, you are mine, you are what

A
A7sus
E
A
you are.
You make it
hard,
and you make it
E
A
E
hard,
and you make it
hard,
A
E
and you make it
hard.

E
F♯m
E
Fri - day eve - ning,
Tues - day morn - ing,
F♯m
E
F♯m/A
E/A
A
Sun - day in the af - ter - noon.
please be gone, I'm tired of you.
A7sus
A
E
What have you got to lose?
1
2
3
Can I

D
A
tell it like it is?
But lis - ten to me, ba - by.
D
G/A
A
A7
It's my heart that's a - suf - f'rin'. It's a - dy - in'. And that's what I have to
E
lose.
F♯m
E
I've got an an - swer.
Will you come see me

F♯m
E
F♯m/A
E/A
A
I'm going to fly a - way.
Thurs - days and Sat - ur - days?
A7sus
A
E
What have I got to lose?
What have you got to lose?
1
2
E

D/E
E
A/E
Chest - nut brown ca - nar - y, ru - by - throat - ed spar -
Voic - es of the an - gels, ring a - round the moon -
Lac - y, lilt - ing lyr - ic, los - ing love, la - ment -

E7
D/E
- row, sing a song, don't be long,
- light, ask - ing me, said she so free,
- ing, change my life, make it right,

F♯m/E
E
1, 2
thrill me to the mar - row.
"How can you catch the spar - row?"
be my la - dy.

3
D/E
C♯m/E
4fr
D/E
C♯m/E
4fr
D/E
C♯m/E
4fr
D/E
C♯m/E
4fr
D/E
C♯m/E
4fr
Bm/E
A
Bm
F♯m
D
E
A
Bm
1
F♯m
D
E
Do do do do do, do do do do do do, do do do do do, do do do do.

2
F♯m D E A Bm F♯m D E A Bm
do do do. Que lin - da me la trai - ga Cu - ba,
sol no tie - ne san - gre a - hi,
F♯m D E A Bm F♯m D E
1 A Bm
la re - i - na de la Mar - Car - i - be.
y que tris - te que no
F♯m D E
2 A Bm F♯m D E A Bm
Cie - lo pue - do va - ya. Oh va! Oh va! Do do do do do, do
F♯m D E A Bm
1 F♯m D E
2 F♯m D E
do do do do do, do do do do do, do do do do. do do do.

Summer Breeze

Words and Music by James Seals and Dash Crofts

D
A
E
lets me know ev - 'ry-thing's al - right.
through the screen and a - cross the floor.
Am7
Bm7
Sum - mer breeze
makes me feel fine,
Am7
G
C/G
blow - in' through the jas - mine in my
mind.
3
G
Gsus
3fr
G
Am7
Sum - mer breeze

Bm7
Am7
makes me feel fine,
blow - in' through the jas - mine in my
G
C/G
G
Gsus
G
1
Em7
Am9
mind.
Em7
Am7
Em7
Am9
Em7
Am7
2
Em7
Am9
Em7
Am7
Sweet days of sum - mer the jas - mine's in bloom,

Em7
Am9
5fr
Em7
Am7
Ju - ly is dressed up and play - ing her tune. When I come
Am7/D
Bm7/E
home from a hard day's work and you're
Am7/D
Bm7/E
wait - in' there not a care in the world.
Amaj7/B
A6/B
E
G
See the smile a - wait - in' in the kitch - en,

D
A
E
Am7
food cook - in' and the plates for two.
G
Feel the arms that reach out to hold me
in the eve - ning when the day is through.
Sum - mer breeze
Bm7
makes me feel fine,
blow - in' through the jas - mine in my

G
C/G
G
Gsus
3fr
G
mind.
Am7
Bm7
Sum - mer breeze
makes me feel fine,
Am7
G
C/G
G
Gsus
3fr
G
blow - in' through the jas - mine in my mind.
Em7
Am7
Em7
Am7
Repeat and Fade

Take Me Home, Country Roads

Words and Music by John Denver, Bill Danoff and Taffy Nivert

F♯m
Life is old there, old - er than the
Dark and dust - y, paint - ed on the
E
trees, young - er than the moun - tains
sky, mist - y taste of moon - shine,
D
A
𝄋
A
grow - in' like a breeze.
tear - drop in my eye.
Coun - try roads,
E
F♯m
take me home to the place

D
I be - long:
West Vir -
A
E
gin - ia,
moun - tain mom - ma.
D
To Coda
A
Take me home,
coun - try roads.
1
2
F♯m
All my
I hear her

E
A
voice in the morn - in' hours she calls me. The
D
A
E
ra - di - o re - minds me of my home far a -
F#m
G
way, and driv - in' down the road I get a
D
A
E
feel - in' that I should have been home yes - ter - day, yes - ter -

E7
D.S. al Coda
CODA
A
day.
Coun - try
roads.
E7
Take me home,
coun - try
A
E7
roads.
Take me home,
A
coun - try roads.

Teach Your Children

Words and Music by Graham Nash

D
must have a code
that you can
A
live by,
and
D
so
be - come your - self,
G7
be - cause the past
D
is just a good - bye.
A

D
Teach your chil - dren
Teach your par - ents
G7
well; their fa - ther's
well; their chil - dren's
D
hell
hell
A
did slow - ly go by.
will slow - ly go by.
And
D
feed then on your
G7
dreams,

D
the one they pick's the one you'll know
A
D
by.
Don't you ev-
G
-er ask them why; if they told you, you would
D
Bm
cry, so just look at them and sigh

A
G
A
To Coda
and know they
D
G
love ___ you.
D
A
D
(Can you
And you

G
hear and do you care?
of ten - der years can't know the
D
A
Do you see, you must be
fears that your el - ders grew by.
D
free to teach your chil - dren?
And so please help them with your
G7
D
You'll be - lieve they'll make a
youth. They seek the truth

A
D.S. al Coda
world that we can live in.)
be - fore they can die.
CODA
D
love you.
G
D
A
D
A5
5fr
D

Tears in Heaven

Words and Music by Eric Clapton and Will Jennings

D/F♯
A/E
E
if I saw you in heav - en?
if I saw you in heav - en?
if I saw you in heav - en?
F♯m
C♯/E♯
Em6
(1., 3.) I must be strong
and car - ry on
(2.) I'll find my way
through night and day
F♯
Bm
'cause I know
I don't be - long
'cause I know
I just can't stay
E7sus
To Coda
A
E/G♯
F♯m
A/E
here in heav - en.
here in heav - en.

1
D/F♯
E7sus
E7
A
2
D/F♯
E7sus
E7
A
C
Bm
Time can bring you down,
Am
D/F♯
G
D/F♯
Em
D/F♯
G
time can bend your knees.
C
Bm
Am
D/F♯
G
D/F♯
Time can break the heart, have you beg - gin' please, beg - gin' please.

E
A
E/G♯
F♯m
F♯m/E
D/F♯
A/E
E
A
E/G♯
F♯m
F♯m/E
D/F♯
A/E
E
F♯m
C♯/E♯
Em6
Be - yond the door
there's peace, I'm sure,

F♯
Bm
E7sus
and I know there'll be no more tears in heav -
A
E/G♯
F♯m
A/E
D/F♯
E7sus
E7
en.
A
D.S. al Coda
CODA
A
E/G♯
F♯m
en.
A/E
D/F♯
E7sus
E7
A
rall.

Vincent
(Starry Starry Night)

Words and Music by Don McLean

D7
G6
eyes that know the dark - ness in my soul. Shad - ows on the
flect in Vin - cent's eyes of Chi - na blue. Col - ors chang - ing
eyes that watch the world and can't for - get. Like the stran - gers that you've
hills, sketch the trees and the
hue, morn - ing fields of
met, the rag - ged men in
Am
daf - fo - dils, catch the breeze and the
am - ber grain, weath - ered fac - es
rag - ged clothes, the sil - ver thorn of
C
D7
win - ter chills, in col - ors on the snow - y lin - en
lined in pain are soothed be - neath the art - ist's lov - ing
blood - y rose, lie crushed and bro - ken on the vir - gin

G
C
G
land.
hand.
snow.
Now I un - der -
Now I un - der -
Now I think I
Am
D7
G
stand
stand
know
what you tried to say to me,
what you tried to say to me,
what you tried to say to me,
Em
Am7
D7
how you suf - fered for your san - i - ty,
how you suf - fered for your san - i - ty,
how you suf - fered for your san - i - ty,
how you tried to set them
how you tried to set them
how you tried to set them
Em
To Coda
A7
Am7
D7
free. They would not lis - ten, they did
free. They would not lis - ten, they did
free. They would not lis - ten, they're not
not know how, _
per - haps they'll lis - ten

1
G
now. Star - ry, star - ry
2
G
now. For they could not
Am7
love you.
D7
But still your love was
G
true,
Em
and when no
Am7
hope was left in sight_ on that
Cm6
3fr
star - ry, star - ry night, you
G
took your life,
F7
as lov - ers of - ten
E7
do. But I
Am7
could have told you, Vin - cent, this

C
D7
G
world was nev - er meant for one as
beau - ti - ful as
you.

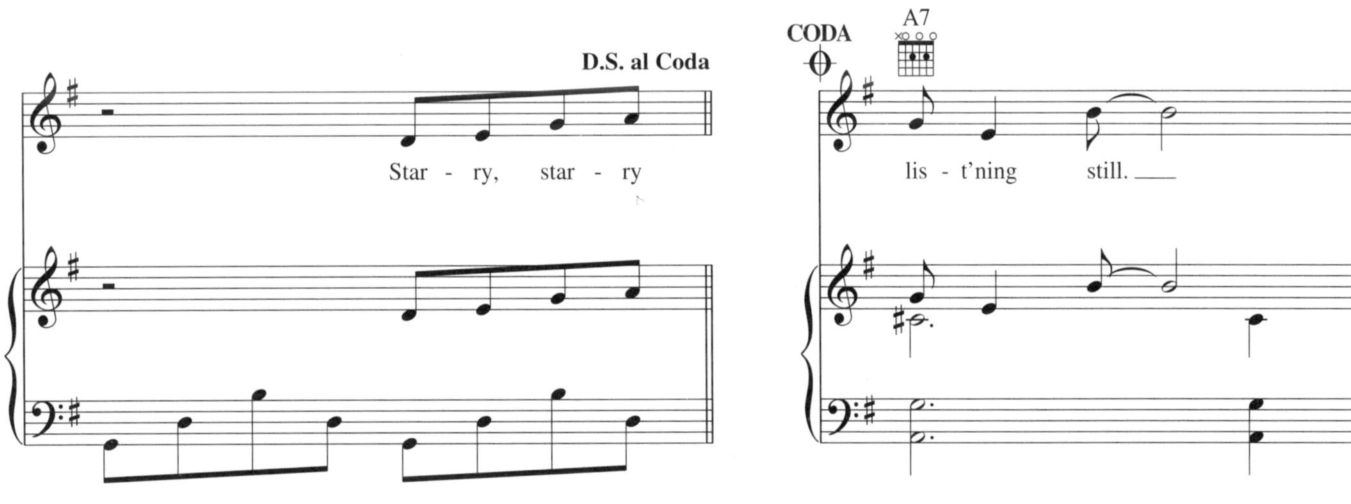
D.S. al Coda
CODA
A7
Star - ry, star - ry
lis - t'ning still.

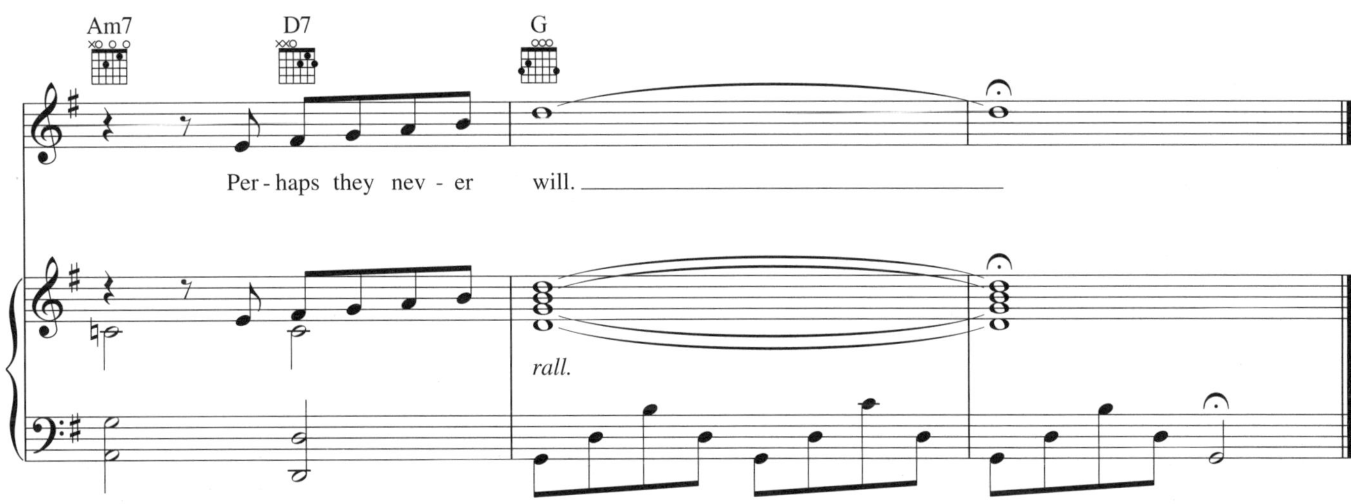
Am7
D7
G
Per - haps they nev - er
will.
rall.

Time in a Bottle

Words and Music by Jim Croce

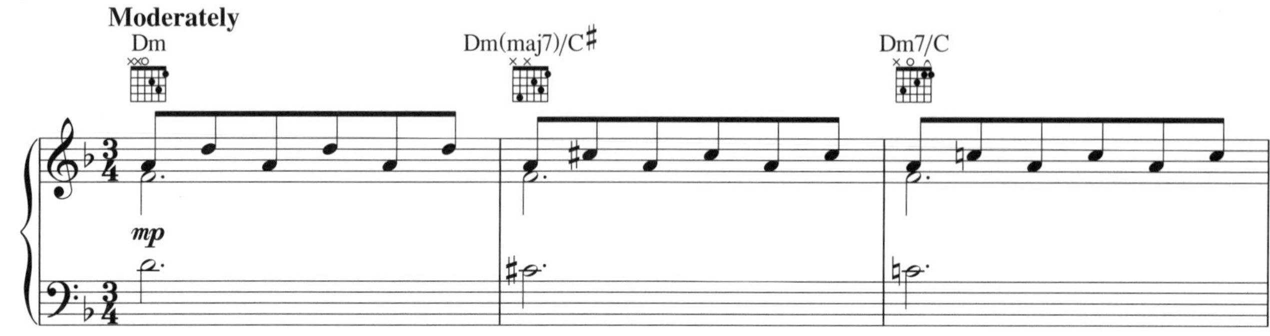

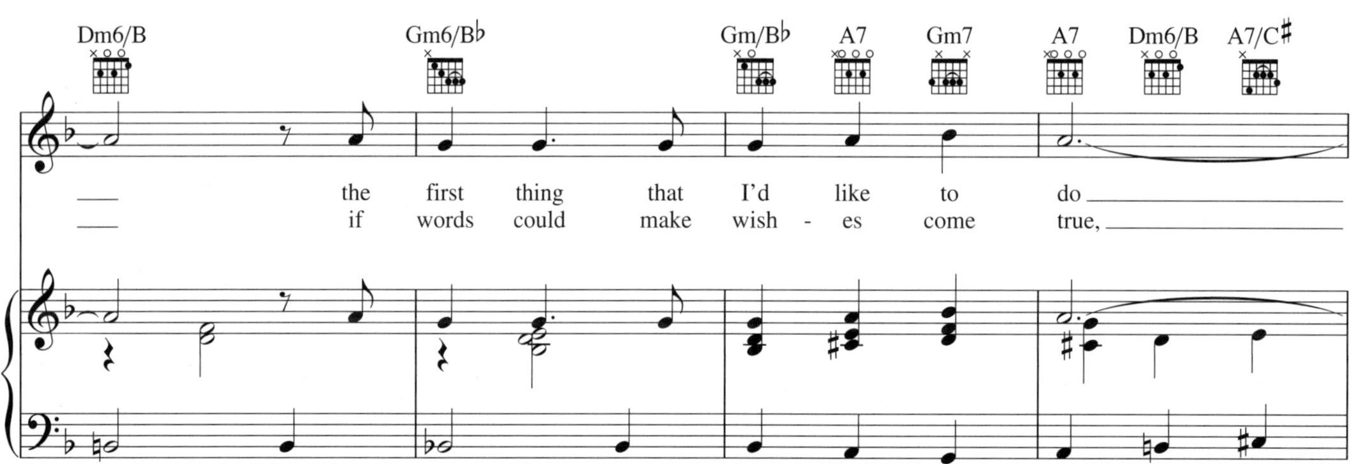

A7/E
Dm
A7/C♯
Dm
Dm7/C
B♭
is to save ev - 'ry day 'til e - ter - ni - ty
I'd save ev - 'ry day like a treas - ure and
Gm7
Dm/F
Gm6
3fr
A7
pass - es a - way just to spend them with you.
then a - gain I would spend them with you.
1
2
D
If
But there nev - er seems to
Dmaj7/C♯
D6/B
D/A
be e - nough time to do the things you want to do once you

G
D6/F♯
Em7
A7
find them.
I've
D
Dmaj7/C♯
D6/B
D/A
looked a - round e - nough to know that you're the one I want to go through
G
D6/F♯
Em7
To Coda
A7
time with.
If
Dm
Dm(maj7)/C♯
Dm7/C
Dm6/B
I had a box just for wish - es and

Gm6/B♭
Gm/B♭
A7
Gm7
A7
Dm6/B
A7/C♯
A7/E
Dm
A7/C♯
dreams that had nev - er come true, the
Dm
Dm7/C
B♭
Gm7
box would be emp - ty ex - cept for the mem - 'ry of
Dm/F
Gm6
3fr
A7
D.S. al Coda
how they were an - swered by you. But there
CODA
A7
Dm
Play 3 times

Turn! Turn! Turn!
(To Everything There is a Season)

Words from the Book of Ecclesiastes
Adaptation and Music by Pete Seeger

G7
C
G
C
F
kill, a time to heal; a time to laugh, a time to weep.
Em
Dm
C
F
Em
Dm
C
F
Em
To ev - 'ry - thing (turn, turn, turn) there is a sea - son (turn, turn,
Dm
F
G
Dm
G
C
turn) and a time for ev - 'ry pur - pose un - der heav - en.
G7
C
G7
A time to build up, a time to break down; a time to dance, a time to

C
G7
C
G
F
Em7
mourn; a time to cast away stones, a time to gath - er stones
G/D
Dm
C
F
Em
Dm
C
F
Em
Dm
to - geth - er. To ev - 'ry - thing (turn, turn, turn) there
C
F
Em
Dm
F
G
Dm
G
is a sea - son (turn, turn, turn) and a time for ev - 'ry pur - pose un - der
C
G7
C
heav - en. A time of love, a time of hate; a time of
A time to gain, a time to lose; a time to

G7
C
G7
C
war, a time of peace; a time you may em - brace, a time to
rend, a time to sew; a time to love, a time to hate; a time for
G
F
G
C
F
Em
Dm
re - frain from em - brac - ing.
peace, I swear it's not too late.
To ev - 'ry -
C
F
Em
Dm
C
F
Em
Dm
F
thing (turn, turn, turn) there is a sea - son (turn, turn, turn) and a
G
Dm
G
1
C
2
C
time for ev - 'ry pur - pose un - der heav - en. heav - en.

Wanted Dead or Alive

Words and Music by Jon Bon Jovi and Richie Sambora

D
Dsus
D
C(add2)
G
all the same,
times I sleep,
Instrumental solo
on - ly the names will change,
some-times it's not for days.
The
C
G
F
D
ev - 'ry day,
peo - ple I meet
it seems we're
al - ways
wast - ing a - way.
go their sep - 'rate ways.
An -
Some -
oth - er place,
times you tell the day
where the
by the
fac - es are so cold,
bot - tle that you drink,
I'd
and
C(add2)
drive all night,
times when you're a - lone,
just to
get back home.
all you do is think.
Solo ends
I'm a

Csus
G
F
D
Csus
G
To Coda
cow-boy, on a steel_ horse._ I ride. I'm want-ed, (want - ed,)
N.C.
D
Csus
G
N.C.
D
dead or a-live._ Want-ed, (want - ed,) dead or a-live._
N.C.
1
Some -

2
D.S. al Coda
Al - right.
CODA
D
N.C.
dead or a - live,
and I walk these streets, a load-ed six-string on my back. I
C(add2)
G7
Csus
3fr
G
F6
D
play for keeps, 'cause I might not make it back. I been
ev - 'ry - where, still I'm stand - ing tall. I've
C(add2)
G

Csus
G
F6
D
seen a mil - lion fac - es
and I've rocked them all,
'cause I'm a
Csus
G
F
D
cow - boy,
on a steel horse. I ride.
I'm
Csus
G
N.C.
D
Csus
G
want - ed, (want - ed,)
dead or a - live.
'Cause I'm a cow - boy,
I got the
F
Dm
C5
G
N.C.
D
night on my side.
I'm want - ed, (want - ed,)
dead or a - live, (dead or a -
3

C5
G
N.C.
D
C5
G
live,) dead or a - live, dead or a - live. I still ride, (I still ride,)
N.C.
D
N.C.
G
N.C.
D
dead or a - live, dead or a - live, dead or a - live,
G
N.C.
N.C.
D
N.C.
dead or a - live, dead or a - live.
D
rit.

You've Got a Friend

Words and Music by Carole King

*Vocal harmony sung 2nd time only

Amaj9
E7sus
- ning, {oh, yeah, ba - by, / oh, yes, I will,} to see you a - gain.
Amaj9
Win - ter, spring, sum - mer or fall,
Dmaj7
F♯m7
D
C♯m
Bm
all you've got to do is call and I'll be there, yeah yeah, yeah;
1
Dmaj7/E
A
D
you've got a friend.

2
D A/C♯ Bm A
G♯m7
C♯7sus
Dmaj7/E
If the sky _ Hey, ain't _
D/G
D
A
Asus
_ it good to know that you've got _ a friend _ when peo - ple can be _ so cold? _
Amaj7
D
Gmaj9
They'll hurt you and de - sert you; well, they'll
F♯m7
B7
Dmaj7/E
take your soul _ if you let _ them, oh yeah, but don't _ you let them.

Amaj9
(Call
out my
name)
You just call
out my name,
and you
Dmaj7
Bm7
E7sus
Amaj9
know wher - ev - er I am
I'll come run - ning
E7sus
to see you a - gain.
Oh, ba - by, don't you know 'bout
Amaj9
Dmaj7
win - ter, spring, sum - mer or fall,
hey now, all you've got to do is call.

F♯m7
Dmaj7
A/C♯
Bm7
Dmaj7/E
Lord, I'll be there, yes, I will, Lord, you've got a friend.
A
D
D/A
A
You've got a friend, yeah.
D
D/A
A
Dmaj7
Ain't it good to know you've got a friend? Ain't it good to know you've got a friend?
D/A
A
D
A/E
A
Oh, yeah, yeah, you've got a friend.

Yesterday

Words and Music by John Lennon and Paul McCartney

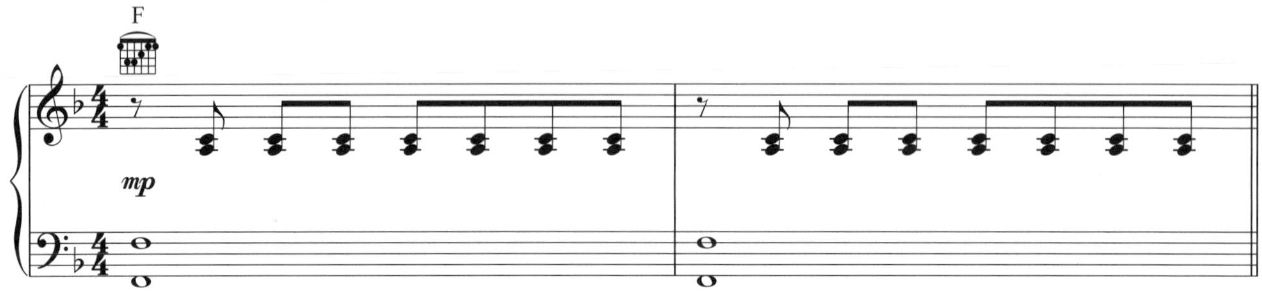

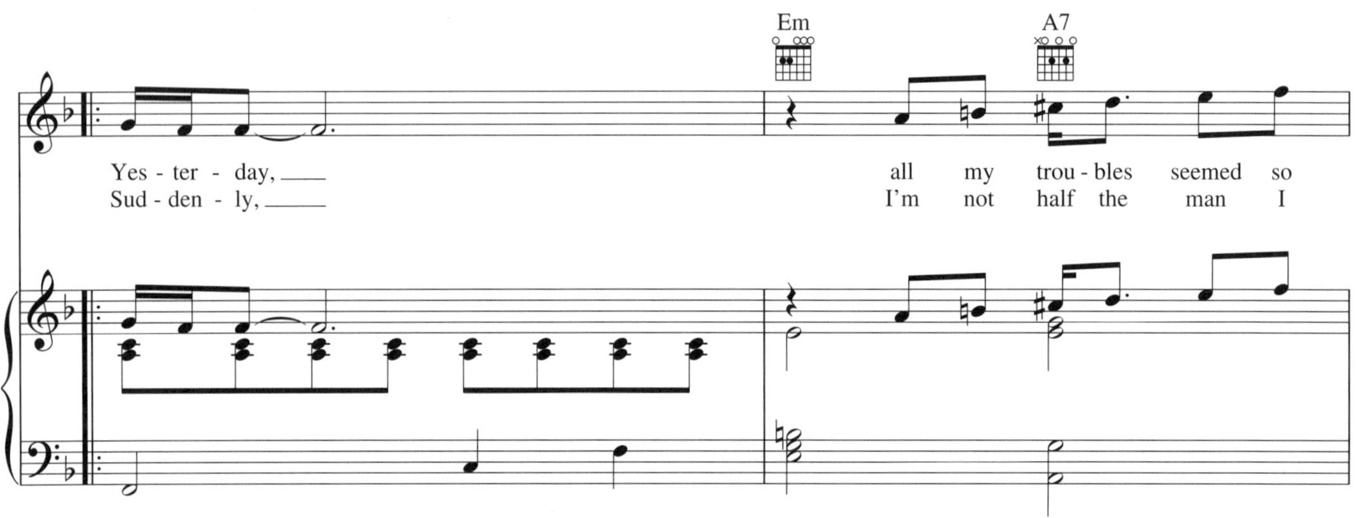

B♭/F F C/E Dm7 G7 B♭ F
here to stay, oh I be - lieve in yes - ter - day.
o - ver me, oh yes - ter - day came sud - den - ly.
G/A A7 Dm C B♭maj7 Dm/A Gm C7
3fr
Why she had to go I don't know, she would - n't say.
G/A A7
I said
Dm C B♭maj7 Dm/A Gm C7 F
some - thing wrong, now I long for yes - ter - day.

Em
A7
Yes - ter - day,
love was such an eas - y
Dm
Dm/C
B♭
C
game to play.
Now I need a place to
B♭/F
F
C/E
Dm7
G7
B♭
F
hide a - way,
oh I be - lieve
in yes - ter - day.
F/C
G/B
B♭
F
Mm mm mm mm
mm mm mm.
rit.